GIPSY WHARF

GIPSY WHARF

(SOJAN BADIAR GHAT)

by

JASIM UDDIN

translated from the Bengali by
Barbara Painter and Yann Lovelock
with illustrations by
Hashem Kahn

London
GEORGE ALLEN AND UNWIN LTD
RUSKIN HOUSE   MUSEUM STREET

UNESCO COLLECTION OF REPRESENTATIVE WORKS
PAKISTAN SERIES

This work
was prepared for
the Pakistan Series
of the Translations Collection
of the United Nations
Educational, Scientific and Cultural Organization
(UNESCO)

PRINTED IN GREAT BRITAIN
in 11 on 12 pt Baskerville
BY UNWIN BROTHERS LIMITED
WOKING AND LONDON

FOREWORD

This translation, which was commissioned by the United Nations Educational, Scientific and Cultural Organization (UNESCO) for the Pakistan Series of its 'Collection of Representative Works', is the fruit of the intimate collaboration of two persons, Mrs Barbara Painter, of the United States, who spent several years in Bengal studying the language and folklore of my people, and of Mr Yann Lovelock, a talented young English poet. Mrs Painter made the first draft of the translation, and then Mr Lovelock, in constant consultation with Mrs Painter, gave it its final form. I would like to express my very deep appreciation to both of them for having given so much of their time and energy and care to making the English version of *Sojan Badiar Ghat* a vivid reflection of the original Bengali.

JASIM UDDIN

CONTENTS

INTRODUCTION

By Barbara Painter

About the Author

In East Pakistan, on the outskirts of the capital city Dacca, is the village Kamlapur. The biggest house in the village is 'Palash Bari', the home of the poet Jasim Uddin; the road leading to it is Jasim Uddin Road. This man is considered by many the foremost living poet of Pakistan. He is respected both at home and abroad, and his books have been translated from Bengali into English, Russian and Czech.

Jasim Uddin knows every facet of village life in Bengal and is partial to rural people. The heroes of his poems and stories are farmers, fishermen, ferrymen, boatmen, weavers, cowherds, even roadside barbers, wandering gipsies, palmists and astrologers. For years he has listened to folk songs and folk tales and in his own poetry has tried to capture the rural manner of speech and thought. In the preface to his longest narrative poem, *Sojan Badiar Ghat* (1933), the title of which Mr Yann Lovelock has rendered *Gipsy Wharf*, Jasim Uddin writes: 'All the people in this book belong to the village. In the speeches of the characters through whom I speak here and there I have added a few lines of folk poetry. In some places I have relied on folk songs such as in the lines "sun and moon be witness".'[1] These lines are spoken by the heroine Duli, 'Be witness sun and moon and all your starry train; be witness righteous gods and all the forest trees and leaves, now and hereafter none shall have my love, but Sojan, captain of my soul',[2] and again by the hero in a later chapter, 'Be witness sun, moon, stars, and gods, how we escape this trap of misery'.[3] Thus in two of the most important events of the

---

[1] Jasim Uddin, *Sojan Badiar Ghat*, Dacca, East Pakistan, Eden Press, 6th ed. 1955. The first edition was published in 1933 probably in Dacca or possibly Calcutta, India .(See below, footnote 34.)

[2] Jasim Uddin, *Gipsy Wharf*, Chapter 10.   [3] *ibid.*, Chapter 21.

book, the elopement and the death of the lovers, he has called on a folk song to aid expression.

Jasim Uddin is proud of belonging to the folk tradition of Bengali literature. He was pleased by a recent comment of one critic who, praising his autobiography, said: 'Reading Jasim Uddin's *Jiban Katha* (autobiography) is like eating country cakes from mother's own hand.'[1] Such a comment on any of the author's other works would please him also. One of Jasim Uddin's early poems about the folk of Bengal is *Nakshi Kathar Math* (1929) which Mrs E. M. Milford translated in 1939 and called *The Field of the Embroidered Quilt*.[2] In many ways this book is a companion piece to *Gipsy Wharf*: the two ballads are the only works of similar plot, construction, and length that he has written. *The Field* has been performed successfully as a dance drama in Dacca and Karachi; *Gipsy Wharf* would also lend itself to this form.

In a foreword to the translation of *Nakshi Kathar Math*, Mr Verrier Elwin writes, 'I do not know whether *The Field of the Embroidered Quilt* can be classed as folk-poetry, but it is obviously poetry about the folk. After nearly ten years of village life I find every detail of the picture, every turn of the story, waking a response in my mind.'[3] What Mr Elwin says of *The Field* can also be said of *Gipsy Wharf*. The two poems were written within four years of each other, while Jasim Uddin was still at Calcutta University, doing research under the famous Bengali scholar, Dr Dinesh Chandra Sen. *Gipsy Wharf* benefited from Dr Sen's comments as well as those of the famous writer and painter Awbanindranath Tagore.[4] Both these men have written or collected Bengali folk literature; Dr Sen was perhaps the foremost authority on the

---

[1] Jasim Uddin, *Jiban Kotha* (autobiography), Part I, Dacca, Polash Publishers, 1964.

[2] Jasim Uddin, *The Field of the Embroidered Quilt*, Calcutta, Oxford University Press, India, 1939. Henceforth I will refer to this oft-cited work simply as *The Field*.

[3] Jasim Uddin, *op. cit.*, p. x. Foreword by Verrier Elwin.

[4] Jasim Uddin, *Sojan Badiar Ghat*, the Preface; 'The honorable Dinesh Chandra Sen and Awbanindranath Tagore, by reading the manuscript of this book, have helped me in many ways. I am very indebted to both of them.'

subject.[1] In an introduction to *The Field*, Dr Sen writes, 'The author's penetrating insight into the very character of our masses, his talented grasp of the characteristics of feminine feelings, have invested the poem with life-like presentation of the moral and cultural traits of Bengalis. . . . It is difficult nowadays to find a faithful picture of Bengal in any of the modern novels and tales. Even our reputed authors are consciously or unconsciously led by Western influence, and the true Bengali whom we meet in our villages is now difficult to meet in literature.'[2]

Jasim Uddin, whether one considers him a folk poet or not, does a very good job of depicting the language and feeling of the folk, and particularly in early works such as *The Field* and *Gipsy Wharf*. At the time of their composition in Bengali he was busy with his research under Dr Sen, collecting folk literature in the villages of East Bengal. He was also composing folk songs of his own. One of the books he published around this period is *Rangila Nayer Majhi* (1930) (Boatman of the Gay Boat). In a preface to this song-book Jasim Uddin writes, 'In search of the speech and mode of expression of the common man of Bengal I have been travelling to many villages for the last fourteen years, collecting many kinds of folk songs.'[3] In those years Jasim Uddin also worked for gramophone companies located in Calcutta who published the songs he collected for them in East Bengal. 'I have made numerous records of folk songs for many Calcutta companies. Among these songs some are of my own composition, some are incomplete compositions of un-educated folk poets that I have collected and revised, and then again some of the fragmentary folk songs I collected I have recorded just as I found them.'[4] At the time of writing

[1] Dr D. C. Sen was for many years the head of the department of Bengali Literature at Calcutta University. One of his favourite projects was the collection of folk literature from the villages. He published several books on the subject; two well-known ones are *Eastern Bengal Ballads*, Calcutta, University of Calcutta Press, 1921, and *The Folk Literature of Bengal*, University of Calcutta Press, 1923.

[2] Jasim Uddin, *The Field*, Introduction, p. vii, D. C. Sen.

[3] Jasim Uddin, *Rangila Nayer Majhi*, 4th ed., Dacca, Saek Monir Uddin and Co., 1954 (1st ed. was *circa* 1930).

[4] Jasim Uddin, *Sojan Badiar Ghat*, 1933, The Preface.

Gipsy Wharf he had immersed himself in a flood of folk songs. At the beginning of each chapter the folk song that inspired it is quoted.[1]

There were influences on Jasim Uddin's writing other than folk songs and ballads. Perhaps that is why some hesitate to call him a folk poet. He is also a scholar and for many years was a lecturer in Bengali literature at Dacca University. Then during the war he became a civil servant and for sixteen years worked for the government. He has travelled in many foreign lands. Even at the time of writing early works such as *The Field* and *Gipsy Wharf*[2] he had read widely in classical Bengali as well as folk literature and was familiar with English literature too. To take *Graves*[2] as an example, Jasim Uddin says he was inspired to write this poem by reading Grey's *Elegy in a Country Churchyard*. The earliest influence on his poetry, however, was a group of minor folk poets of Bengal. He mentions them as his first teachers: 'From Rabindranath [Tagore] on down many critics have said the flow of my verse is very easy. If that is a virtue then I have learned this from our country's uneducated and half-educated poets. They are the first teachers of my poetic life, the poets Jadab, Parikshit, Ismail, Hari Patani and Hari Acharya. Into every rural household of Bengal they have poured an immortal flow of nectar. Deprived of that the Bengali heart would be a dry wasteland.'[3]

If Jasim Uddin's writing has benefited from influences other than these rustic poets of Bengal, that has in no way made him less an expert on Bengali village life. At least at the time of writing *Gipsy Wharf* he was very much involved with the villages of East Bengal and the poem might even be considered a direct outcome of his experiences with them. Though it is fiction and somewhat in the romantic vein, the

[1] In Mr Lovelock's opinion the Western reader cannot respond to the folk-song epigraphs, expressing the spirit of the chapters which they head, in the same way as a Bengali who is familiar with them. He has accordingly added epigraphs from other literary traditions, with which the reader may be more familiar, by way of contrast. (See pp. 190–1.) The non-Bengali poems are given in italics.

[2] *Kobor*, another poem written about this time (1929) will be found in Appendix I under the title *Graves*.

[3] Jasim Uddin, *Jiban Kotha*, Part I, 1964, Dacca, Polash Publishers, p. 122.

substance of the book is the village life as he saw it round about him. The poet asserts he gathered material for his plot from actual happenings in his own Faridpur district. 'In our Faridpur district there live many poor farmers, Moslem and Namasudra (Hindus). Almost continuously there is a quarrel among them over some insignificant incident. In all these quarrels the wealthy Hindus and Moslems encourage them and drive them down the path of disaster. Among the rich and the landlords there is no distinction of caste. In the world of the exploiters all are of one class. If one could see the condition these unfortunate Namasudras and Moslems are left in by the oppression of these people, one could not hold back tears from one's eyes. With just such incidents the plot of this book is constructed.'[1]

Jasim Uddin was born on January 1, 1903, in a small village, Tambulkhana, in the Faridpur district of East Bengal. That was his grandparents' village, only eight miles from his parents' home in Govindapur. He has described these two villages and their manner of life in his auto-biography. Many scenes from *The Field* and *Gipsy Wharf* have their setting in these villages. In those books Jasim Uddin is writing of a time when the land of Bengal had fewer problems than present-day East Pakistan, with its overpopulation, influx of refugees, chronic floods, epidemics and food short-ages. He likes even now to think of those happier days, and writes: 'In every household there were milk cows. Those who did not have cows could go to a neighbour's house and ask for milk. Sitting on my blind great uncle Danu Mullah's lap as a boy, I used to listen to these stories of ease and prosperity. In my books *Nakshi Kathar Math* (The Field) and *Sojan Badiar Ghat* (Gipsy Wharf) I was remembering the peoples of these villages. Even today this picture of plenty in the villages gives me pleasure when I think about it. If I could but change this joyless, needy land of today with all its prejudice for that land of happiness, song and pros-perity, I would dance for joy.'[2]

It is the picture of the contented farmer living on his fertile

---

[1] Jasim Uddin, *Sojan Badiar Ghat*, 1933, the Preface.
[2] Jasim Uddin, *Jiban Kotha*, pp. 16–17.

land that gives Jasim Uddin the most pleasure. The heroes
in his books either are farmers, such as the boy Rupa in *The
Field*, or the illiterate hero of his novel *Boba Kahini*, or like
Sojan of *Gipsy Wharf* they want to be farmers. Though his
own father did not have much land Jasim Uddin had the
satisfaction of knowing that many of his ancestors were
prosperous Bengali farmers. He writes of one in particular,
a certain Aradhan Mullah, 'I have heard that Aradhan
Mullah was a large land-holder in the village. He was very
well to do. He owned fields full of sugar cane. When this cane
was cut the stalks were crushed and juice extracted; the juice
was boiled into syrup. The vendors used to carry thousands
and thousands of pounds of this syrup in pots hung from
shoulder yokes. When they passed through the village carry-
ing it from Aradhan Mullah's house to the markets and
bazaars, the village ladies used to come out of their houses
to watch. A guest or traveller was never turned away from
that house. Stored in his counting house were huge baskets
full of fried rice, sweetened rice and coconut confections.
Whoever wished could come and eat. Sometimes at his house
as many as two or three hundred people would eat with his
family.'[1]

It was a land of plenty in those days with no need for much
money or hard work. One might say Laksmi, the goddess of
wealth, smiled on Bengal. 'In former days, in every quarter
of the village there were song gatherings, *Gajir* songs, *Jari*
songs and *Keccha* songs,[2] which kept the villages in a state of
excitement. The fields yielded good harvests. With a little
scraping of the plough and a flick of the wrist to sow the
seed broadcast, green sprouts appeared covering the paddy
fields as far as the horizon. The rivers, canals and ponds
swarmed with fish. One had only to scoop them out by hand.
Very few things were bought with money. For a few sheaves
of paddy the blacksmith would forge a plough, the barber
would cut hair, the potter make pots; for a little mustard seed

[1] Jasim Uddin, *Jiban Kotha*, p. 17.
[2] *Gajir*, *Jari* and *Keccha* songs are group songs, with perhaps a leading singer
narrating the story and a dancer acting it as it is sung. *Gajir* means a moslem
warrior, *Jari* a group, and *Keccha* a story.

the oil presser would deliver mustard oil to every home. Even now this method of barter is in use in the villages.'[1]

These recollections of a happier land, told Jasim Uddin by his blind relative, are, perhaps, doubly attractive to the poet because of the needs of the overpopulated hungry land today and because as a boy Jasim Uddin knew what it was to be hungry. He writes, 'When I was a boy I had no fine clothes to wear. I did not have winter clothes sometimes, but I do not think that I felt any particular sorrow on that account. For no other thing do I blame my mother and father except that, when I was a growing boy, I was driven to seek out those sweet and wholesome foods my body required, looking in the forests and jungles for this or that fruit. When at someone's house rice cakes were being made the housewife would give them to her own boys and girls, then to everyone else. I used to hope after one plate was empty she would ask me to have a cake; one plate was empty, then another. Still the housewife did not look at me. So, heaving a great sigh, I returned home.'[2]

For, when Jasim Uddin was a boy, his family was very poor. His father was the teacher in the village school, a very dedicated man who sometimes earned only seven rupees a month. Later he became the mullah, the religious leader of the Moslem community in the village. In Jasim Uddin's own words, 'My father's uncle, Jahir Uddin Mullah, was the mullah of our village. For some reason or other he left the country to go to Malda (a village in West Bengal near Calcutta), and the responsibility for the office of mullah fell on my father.... If there were a wedding among the farmers of the village father would receive from one to three rupees. ... In the estimation of the village, father now held a position of leadership.'[3]

Jasim Uddin's mother brought her family through some difficult days. She was the only woman in the house, which is unusual in Bengal. There were no grandmothers, spinster aunts or other female relations to help her with the house-work. When his mother, Ranga-chhutu, wanted to make the rice cakes the boy Jasim was so fond of, she rose before dawn

---

[1] Jasim Uddin, *Jiban Kotha*, p. 17.   [2] *ibid.*, p. 55.   [3] *ibid.*, p. 14.

to husk the paddy. When she went to the cooking shed her son sometimes accompanied her. He would sit near her waiting for the first rice cakes to be ready. There is a compliment he pays her cooking, 'To myself I kept praising my mother. My mother knows so much. Receiving the magic touch of my mother's hand, the bits of rice and treacle would become such delicious rice cakes and be transformed into something new. This is the task of every artist. He takes what he has to work with and, manipulating it according to his liking, gives it new life.'[1]

Jasim Uddin's mother came from the village of Tambulkhana. Though only eight miles from the larger village Govindapur, Tambulkhana was almost in the jungle. Jasim Uddin writes of it, 'I have heard long ago there was no jungle in that place. The prosperous farmers lived in well-built bungalows. The village teemed with people. Then there was a cholera epidemic and many fell sick with malaria as well. Where an orchard once flourished, bamboo and vines and creepers began to grow so thickly they made the spot unfit for human habitation. Then jackals, polecats, wild boar, tigers and other animals gradually made their home there. The farmers who did not move their houses and goods far away had to fight a continuous battle with the wild beasts.'[2] While on a visit to Tambulkhana as a boy, he recalls how a tiger came one night and prowled around their cottage. This village of his grandparents was an exciting place. He enjoyed accompanying his mother there, walking alongside her bearer-born palanquin down the jungle paths.

In spite of his poverty, Jasim Uddin spent an interesting childhood. Recalling those days he writes, 'I look back as far as my gaze will go to the first scenes of the far past of my life. In that land of light and shadow some things are clear, some hazy; a few pictures come floating to my mind. On a rainy day, having spread an embroidered quilt on the floor, mother is sitting there sewing. She is humming a tune. . . . Father, rising before dawn, is reciting the prayers. From his throat the intonation made an incomparable impression on my half-asleep boy's mind such that I can never express

---

[1] Jasim Uddin, *Jiban Kotha*, p. 48.   [2] *op. cit.*, p. 45.

18

in words. . . . Standing at the door is a *fakir* who wears a string of fiery beads around his neck. He is singing from the book of Joseph and Zuleka. . . . After I had played the whole day, and my body was covered with mud and earth, I would return home at sundown. Catching hold of me, mother would wipe me clean with her own sari. . . . Across the whole sky a storm was raging. Thunder crashed with loud peals. Lying in bed I clasped my arms around father's neck. . . . All day there was a cloudy sky. Light rain was falling continuously. In the reception room of the landlord, uncle was reciting from a book. I had not yet reached the age to understand what he was intoning. The sound of the recitation mixed with that of the falling rain brought some kind of detached feeling to my mind. . . . And just such very small memories come to my mind like pictures. Many very important happenings I have forgotten; but when I find time these pictures come and play on the theatre stage of my thought.'[1] Jasim Uddin has woven some of these memories into his writing. The heroine of *The Field of the Embroidered Quilt* sews her story on just such a home-made village quilt. In Chapter 4 of *Gipsy Wharf* the ghosts scatter and the boy Sojan is awakened from his dream by the morning call to prayer.

In his autobiography Jasim Uddin tells much more about village life as he knew it. He swam in the ponds and canals, fished in the rainy season, watched the sugar cane being made into treacle, and ate his fair share of this tasty sweet. The boy Jasim built a banana-palm raft and sailed it one early morning to help himself to a neighbour's ripe dates. Like his hero Sojan, he knew where the weaver bird made its nest and admired the intricate construction. He knew when and where the best mangoes and plums were ripe. When the travelling theatre, the *Jatra*, came to town he and his cousin, Nehaj Uddin, would sneak off and stay up all night listening to the play. Throughout the year they enjoyed both the Hindu and the Moslem holidays.

In most ways his life as a boy in Bengali villages was like that of other boys. He had, however, a most unusual friend, a Hindu ascetic, a *sannyasi*. The *sannyasi* came one day and made

<hr>

[1] Jasim Uddin, *Jiban Kotha*, pp. 1 and 2.

his hermitage (called an *asram*) on the outskirts of Govindapur near the Hindu cremation *ghat*. Soon this holy man had many followers, but none more ardent than the small Moslem boy, Jasim. He listened attentively to the *sannyasi* reading the Hindu scriptures. He took pleasure in tending the flower garden which surrounded the little *asram*, a necessary adjunct as flowers are used in worshipping the gods. He even cleaned the *asram*. The *sannyasi* in turn taught the boy the Hindu scriptures which, like the Bible, are full of exciting stories. He taught him many disciplines and meditations; one which Jasim Uddin mentions practising was how to overcome sensitivity to cold. The boy was very devoted to this *guru* (teacher), and when the *sannyasi* left the village to make a pilgrimage to the Himalayas, Jasim was very disappointed that he could not accompany him.

Although he later gave up any belief in the Hindu gods, Jasim Uddin believes he cannot over-emphasize the influence of the *sannyasi* in his life and his debt to the good man. He writes, 'Now I have no belief in mother Kali or other gods and goddesses. Nor do I believe in being disciple to a *guru*. But from my boyhood to the present day for the love and affection which I received from the *sannyasi* there remains a love and respect in my heart which has not in the least bit been destroyed.'[1] In another passage Jasim Uddin writes, 'Whether hearing that long tale of the *sannyasi* will be of benefit to anyone I do not know. I am no longer a follower of that path along which he was a traveller. His gods and methods or worship are not my religion today.'[2]

For the friendship of the *sannyasi* and the insight he gave him into Hindu culture, Jasim Uddin is still grateful. It seems to me his broadmindedness and sympathy for Hindu as well as Moslem tradition are among his best qualities as a writer. *Gipsy Wharf* is almost a plea for better Hindu–Moslem relations. Certainly he believes that the bonds which unite Bengali people are very strong, and the culture they have made is both Hindu and Moslem. Thanking the *sannyasi* in another passage, Jasim Uddin writes, 'When I must give up something today it is not difficult for me to do so. Besides

[1] Jasim Uddin, *Jiban Kotha*, pp. 170–1.   [2] *ibid.*, p. 172.

this discipline, the knowledge I obtained when a boy, of the Hindu gods and goddesses, of the method of accomplishing tasks that at first seem impossible, has helped me immensely in my creative work. The literature of this land (Bengal) is not merely Hindu literature, nor can it be said to be a Moslem literature. Since both Hindus and Moslems have written in one language (Bengali), the literature of this land is both Hindu and Moslem. Those who would separate the two and make literature will not last many days, I am sure. Because of the universality of appeal in the world of literature, sectarian thought is out of place there. If my own writing has achieved anything of universal appeal, then it is thanks to that *sannyasi*.'[1]

The *sannyasi* probably had the strongest influence of any person outside his family on Jasim Uddin. The boy did, however, have other friends who helped him, particularly with his poetry. His interest began when he was very young, perhaps seven or eight years old. He writes, 'Once I went to Shamsundarpur for my uncle's wedding. This village was almost six miles from our village. On the following morning I rose early and in the distance heard the sound of drumming. When I asked about this I learned that in the neighbouring zamindar's estate-office there was a ballad recitation[2] in progress, and the sound of the drum-beat was coming from there. I followed the sound of the drums and gradually came closer to the estate-office. As I approached I heard also the indistinct tone of singing along with the drums. That tune drew me as in a dream towards the ballad recital.'[3]

All during the uncle's wedding procession the lines from the song recital kept running through his mind. As he walked along with the rest of the wedding party, escorting his bridegroom uncle's palanquin up and down the winding roads to the bride's house, the small boy sang aloud snatches from the ballad recitation he had heard. When he returned to his own village he sought out one of the local poets to

---

[1] Jasim Uddin, *Jiban Kotha*, p. 173.
[2] Jasim Uddin notes that the verses were composed *extempore*, and that the local bards were here in competition.
[3] *ibid.*, p. 113.

engage in a little song contest like that he had heard at the estate-office. He writes, 'I have spoken before of Rahim Molak of the weaver's quarter. Because he is a man of my village I call him uncle. He can compose ballads with little effort. Early one morning I went to see him and said, "Uncle, I want to have a ballad contest with you." '[1] So the weaver put aside his work and had a contest with the little boy. The weaver composed a ballad which consisted mostly of jokes about things that happened in the village. Then the boy Jasim sang snatches from what he heard at the recital, adding his own lines to that.

At the time of the contest with the weaver Jasim Uddin had no idea he was composing poetry. He was reciting what he had heard and adding his own words in the same tune. He says of that time, 'It was still my belief that books and poetry, like earth and sky, were there from the beginning or else God Himself had created them. Could man make such things!'[2]

When he discovered that he was composing poetry Jasim Uddin made some effort to write it in a notebook. At first he had some difficulty: 'I had heard that poems had fourteen syllables in every line, and in the first line of a couplet the last syllable rhymed with the last syllable of the second line. Taking up pen and paper I thought and thought but could go no further. Sitting on the river bank I remained gazing at the sand bank on the other shore, but I could not compose a fourteen syllable line. Now and then I was so angry I tore my hair.

'One day it suddenly occurred to me; how would it be if I wrote the words in my notebook in the same ready manner that I composed oral poetry? After writing three or four of my couplets in the notebook I was astonished. There were fourteen syllables in every line and the last syllable of every line rhymed with the second line's last syllable. I doubt whether Columbus discovering America felt such joy as I felt at this discovery. For so many days I was accustomed to composing my verse to a tune. Without a tune I could not

[1] Jasim Uddin, *Jiban Kotha*, p. 114.
[2] *ibid.*, p. 119.

22

compose the words in poetical metre. Now that I discovered
how to find the rhythm for my verse, who could hold me back?
I filled notebook after notebook.'[1]

There were other friends who helped the boy with his
poetry. He has mentioned that his first teachers were the
rural poets Jadab, Ismail, etc. A later teacher was Pandit
Khirad Babu. 'With Khirad Babu I used to go for a walk
by the river almost every evening. The two of us sat there
watching the sun set . . . on the return path he gave me varied
advice on the composition of poetry.'[2]

Still another teacher Jasim Uddin mentions is Madhu
Pandit: 'I only remember something he said one day. I had
asked the Pandit, "I want to write Bengali books. You give
me some good advice. What shall I do to succeed in this?"
Laughing he replied, "You are a Bengali boy. Whatever you
write will be Bengali. For that there is nothing you need do.
Whatever you have to say, write it in the same manner as
you are talking to me. That will be your best composition."
All my life I have tried to apply the advice of this pandit to
my work.'[3]

So, at the age of eight he started composing his own poetry.
When he was still a young lad he visited a dramatics club in
Faridpur: 'Watching the theatre rehearsals over and over
I learned some of the passages of the plays by heart. Standing
by the riverside in the evening I would recite them in a loud
voice. People used to call me mad Jasim. In this manner,
reciting one play after another, my weak voice became quite
strong. I also learned the art of raising and lowering my voice
effectively.'[4] Many times the boy did not have the money to
pay for a theatre ticket, but he found a way to see the show:
'Climbing the betel tree, shivering and trembling in the cold,
I used to watch the play. In this manner I saw the plays
Shah Jahan, *The Moghul Pathan*, *Shonay Shohaga* (A Happy
Marriage), *Raja Harish Chandra* and others. Now and then
by hook or crook I got a pass for one or two days' performance.
On those days I tried to memorize the whole of the play.
Going to the river bank the next day I recited my lines like

[1] Jasim Uddin, *Jiban Kotha*, p. 121.　　[2] *ibid.*, p. 122.
[3] *ibid.*, p. 123.　　[4] *ibid.*, p. 135.

the characters in the play.'[1] It appears that Jasim Uddin
had the makings of an actor as well as a poet. In later years,
when he was a civil servant, he used to make speeches for the
government in the villages and proved such a good speaker
that his audience of village people numbered thousands.

Thus Jasim Uddin started reciting and composing poems at
a very early age. By the time he was a student at Faridpur
Rajendra College his poetry had already won him some fame.
Kobor (Graves) was prescribed as the text for the Matricula-
tion Examination at Calcutta University when Jasim Uddin
was still a student in the I. A. Class for collecting ballads and
folk songs. Though Jasim Uddin says it was inspired by Gray's
Elegy in a Country Churchyard, this poem is Bengali in content
and an innovation; nothing like it had been written in Bengali
literature before. It was around this time that he was writing
Nakshi Kathar Math (The Field), and four years later he had
published *Sojan Badiar Ghat* (Gipsy Wharf).

Gipsy Wharf and *The Field*, I think, are among Jasim
Uddin's major work, but he is a versatile and prolific writer.
Like another famous Bengali poet, Rabindranath Tagore,
Jasim Uddin has tried his pen in almost every field. *Boba
Kahini* (Tale of an illiterate man) 1964 is his only novel. He has
written many short dance dramas: *Beder Meye* 1951 (The
Gipsy Girl), *Madhumala* 1956 (from the fairy tale of Princess
Madhumala), *Palli Badhu* (Village Bride) 1956, the plot of
which, he writes, is borrowed from Tagore. Jasim Uddin has
also collected and rewritten numerous folk tales. He has
published two volumes *Bangalar Hashir Galpa* (Laughing
Tales of Bengal), vol. 1, 1961, vol. 2, 1964.

Among Jasim Uddin's song books, perhaps the best are
Rangila Nayer Majhi (Boatman of the Gay Boat) 1933 and
Padma Par (The Banks of the Padma River) 1949. Foremost of
his lyrics are the books *Rakhali* (Pastoral Poems) 1929, *Balu
Char* (The Sandbank) 1930, *Dhan Khet* (The Paddy Field)
1932. Other important lyrics written recently are in the books
Rupavati 1946 and *Sakhina* 1960 (both girl's names). The first
book of lyrics published after the partition of India–Pakistan,
when the poet moved permanently to Dacca, was the book

[1] Jasim Uddin, *Jiban Kotha*, p. 134.

Matir Kanna (Sorrows of the Earth) 1955. This book has been translated into Russian.[1]

Jasim Uddin has travelled to the United States and to many countries of Europe. In the Orient he has visited Burma and Indonesia, and most recently China. After many of these travels he wrote articles which found their way eventually into books such as *Chale Musafir* (The Traveller) 1961, *Jader Dekhechi* (Those I have seen) and *Halde Parir Deshe* (In the Land of the Yellow Fairy) 1965, a book about Yugoslavia which was awarded a prize by Unesco. He has also written a book on his experiences with the famous Tagore family, particularly with the painter Awbanindranath Tagore, called *Thakur Barir Anginay* (In the Courtyard of the Tagores). There is also a collection of his lyrics, *Shuchaiyani* (Selected Poems) 1961. Part I of his autobiography *Jiban Kotha* (Life Story) was published in 1964. He is presently working on Part II and it will presumably reveal much more of interest about his full life.

One of the books that has been translated into other languages, *Matir Kanna*, was reviewed by the writer Syed Ali Ashraf who made these interesting comments: 'Jasim Uddin, the most successful ballad writer of Pakistan, has published only one book of poems since partition, *Matir Kanna* . . . Jasim Uddin has always written about primitive village folk and their natural sufferings. The only thing that appears to be new is that he has accepted the fashion of rebellion against the social conventions which he thinks are the causes of all miseries. . . . He was a pioneer in introducing rural imagery into Bengali literature but has not contributed anything new in the present book. . . . While in his former long ballads he used to write about the common people as one who has lived their life, in his new poems he writes as a sympathizer from outside, one who is sentimentally moved to shed a few tears

[1] Even the Library of Congress does not have dates for the first editions of some of Jasim Uddin's early lyrics. From his book *Shuchaiyani* (Selected Poems) 1961, undated first editions of books such as *Rangila Nayer Majhi* and *Dhan Khet* can be placed fairly accurately from their position in this chronological selection the poet has made of his own lyrics. Who the publishers of *Sojan Badiar Ghat* were in the first edition 1933 I have not discovered. In the 6th edition they are Eden Press, Dacca, East Pakistan, 1955.

for the poor souls. . . . I feel that Jasim Uddin's imaginative capacity is still unimpaired, but he has probably forgotten to devote himself to the realization of new experiences. He has grown too accustomed to his surroundings, so he has lost the sharpness of his sensation.'[1]

While these remarks on *Matir Kanna* were somewhat critical, obliquely they pay a compliment to Jasim Uddin's only two ballads, *Gipsy Wharf* and *The Field of the Embroidered Quilt*. At least in his boyhood days, Jasim Uddin lived the life of the common people, the folk of East Bengal. I think he will be remembered best where he succeeds in identifying himself with these people, in such poems as *The Field* and *Gipsy Wharf* and, among others, that poem of his student days *Kobor* (Graves), the translation of which is given in Appendix I.

The Story

The story of *Gipsy Wharf* is set in a village in East Bengal during the 1920s. In some ways the plot of this long narrative poem can be compared to Shakespeare's *Romeo and Juliet*. The hero, Sojan, is the son of a Moslem farmer; the heroine, Dulali, daughter of the village headman, a Hindu of the Namasudra caste. Their love inevitably leads to a violent clash between the two communities and inexorably to death to themselves.

The poem opens as the headman's daughter is wandering in the woods picking flowers. It describes the idyllic childhood of the two friends and the beauty of their Bengali village. The poet is a lover of rural life and his story captures his own experiences in the villages of Faridpur district, East Bengal. There, for generations, Hindus and Moslems lived peacefully side by side. Jasim Uddin believes Bengali culture is the joint product of these two ethnic groups, and it is the charm of this culture he tries to portray in this story.

Even in the 1920s, Hindus and Moslems did not live without

---

[1] Syed Ali Ashraf, 'Contemporary Poetry and Prose Fiction in East Pakistan' (from *Literary Scene in East Pakistan*, pp. 38–9, published by P.E.N., 1955). It should be mentioned that Jasim Uddin indignantly rejects this interpretation of his work.

friction. To illustrate how trouble might arise from a minor incident he stages a quarrel at the *Maharam* festival in Simul Toli village. A few out-of-town Moslems attack some Simul Toli Namasudras. These Hindus take their grievance to the most prominent man in the village, Nayeb, rent collector for their district.

Nayeb is the villain. All the ills of the zamindary system and the age-long oppression of the Bengali farmer are personified in him. It is his intrigues that finally bring the low caste Sudras and the Moslem community into conflict. Ram Nagar, the local landlord, Nayeb's employer, wants to evict both the Namasudras and the Moslems from Simul Toli so he can use their land to erect a new market. With intrigue and threats and using the elopement of the Moslem boy, Sojan, and the Hindu girl, Dulali, to arouse the Namasudras, he achieves his purpose of stirring up trouble. A fierce battle develops between the two communities, and many die. In the end both Hindus and Moslems suffer great losses and gain nothing. The villain, however, does not go unpunished. He is executed by the joint efforts of the Namasudra headman, Gadai Murul, and the Moslem fencer, Chamir Lethel.

Sojan and Dulali were destined from the beginning to be ill-starred lovers. It is not acceptable for them to marry outside their fellow religions and elopement into the forest seems the only solution. For some time they live happily in their forest cottage, but eventually Sojan is caught and imprisoned. Dulali is remarried by her orthodox parents to a farmer in a distant village. When Sojan is released from jail he finds his family gone, his village disrupted and his beloved remarried. In despair he joins a band of wandering water gipsies. These gipsies have a unique way of living still practised today in East Bengal. Jasim Uddin captures something of their dash, colour and freedom which contrasts strongly with the traditional, formalized pattern of village life.

Sojan's personal tragedy and the sufferings of his community run parallel. In his wanderings with the gipsies, Sojan has been living in the hope of finding Dulali. When he finds her in the water-side village happily remarried, she at first rebuffs him for seeking her out. Then her love for him proves too strong. She steals away in the night, and rejoins Sojan, only to find that his grief at her cold reception has led him to take poison. She takes poison too and the lovers die like Romeo and Juliet. The two communities, however, do not embrace each other because of this tragedy, although Jasim Uddin's wish is certainly that one day Bengalis, Hindu and Moslem, will live as brothers.

THE CAST

Principal characters

SOJAN, a Moslem boy, son of farmer Chamir Shekh
DULALI (DULI), a Hindu girl of the Namasudra (Namu)
    caste
GADAI MURUL, Headman of Simul Toli village, father of
    Dulali
HIS WIFE
NAYEB, rent collector for Ram Nagar, the zamindar
    (landlord) of Simul Toli
MANIR MITRA, Mullah of Simul Toli (= Munshi Saheb)
CHAMIR LETHEL, a renowned Moslem fencer
KALA CHAD RAI, a farmer of Namasudra castle, Dulali's
    husband
THE BOATMAN MINSTREL (who concludes the story)

Villagers of Simul Toli

Namasudras:
    Bindu, a barber
    Nitai, a washerman
    Dukhi Ram, a woodsman
    Kanai Ram, a fisherman
    Ram, a palanquin bearer

Moslems:
    Boda-Ruddi, an oil man, skilled fencer
    Madan Miya, champion fencer

    Dolu ⎫
    Rohim ⎬ participants at Maharam games
    Jaga ⎭

Khan family of Saud-Para village ⎫ Moslems attacking
Sheik family of Bhajanpur village ⎬ Namus at Maharam

Madan Kulu, oil man
Kalimaddi, bearer
Ali-mamud, farmer
Chadan Moral ⎫
Kazem ⎪
Chadam ⎪
Bachan Mitra ⎬ renowned fighters
Ram hati ⎪
Nidhi-Ram ⎪
Mahan Ray ⎭

GIPSY WHARF

CHAPTER I[1]

Let's have some fun, let's have a guessing game;
You show me, if you can, dear, four black things.

Black as the crow, the cuckoo and the fing,
And blacker still, sweet maiden, is your hair.

—Nursery rhyme.

I am black but comely, O ye daughters of Jerusalem.

Behold, thou art fair, my love, behold, thou art fair;
Thou art all fair, my love, there is no spot in thee.

—Solomon's *Song of Songs.*

I saw the headman's dark-skinned daughter once
Walking through brakes of blossomed cane, and heard
The restless ceaseless rustling of the flowers.
Such hues she has as kernels of the grain
Shaken from nodding tips in paddy fields,
The parrot's perch. Put her in durba grass,[2]

[1] *Chapter 1* is particularly difficult for a Westerner to appreciate since much of the charm of the original lies in its language and style, which imitate those of Bengali fairy tales, to which several allusions are made. The use of language is both precocious and intricate. In the first place there is a good deal of peasant vocabulary, to which Jasim Uddin is much given. So much so that he often has to provide a glossary at the end of his poems for his own readers. Secondly, there is a great deal of repetition and word-play which is very difficult to render convincingly in English. For example, the first verse in Bengali runs thus:

Itol-betol fuler bone fhul jhur jhur kore re bhai, fhul jhur jhur kore.
(In the flowering cane-brakes where the flowers flutter and fall, flutter and fall.)

Jhur jhur, a repetition in itself, represents the soft sound of rain falling and derives from the verb *jhoriya*, to fall.

[2] *Durba grass* is a soft dark-coloured grass. A pun is made here since 'durba' means dark-coloured and may be used by itself to refer to this particular type of grass. Thus a literal rendering of the Bengali would be: 'If she were put in a meadow of Durba she would mingle with durba.' The English text puns on the two meanings of 'shade', colouring and shadow.

Her shade would mingle with its shadow dark
To dark; or lay her sleeping on a couch
Of clouds, you'd not distinguish her light form.
As tendrilled gourd leaves[1] soften in the sun
Her swaying body sensuously melts
At its caress, twining the vines of gourd.
Wild creepers in the wood, each branch aflower,
Do not compare with her dark loveliness.
Her path is like a corridor of clouds
Where lightning colours laugh, and rainbows smile
As her flashing sari weaves about her form.

She wears few ornaments, wristlets of glass,
Bell-metal[2] anklets ringing as she walks;
Silver and gold grow pale, are put to shame
By beauty when they seek to heighten it.
She has no need of more who has herself
And passing turns all eyes to look again;
Her slender body, hands, eyes, ears and lips
Are jewels enough to hang about her form.

See her circling lightly as she pleases
Like the verses of the measles puja,[3]
Passing hither, thither, everywhere to pluck
A fruit branch, gather flowers, suck sugar cane.
Perhaps you'll find her with her many dolls,
Singing their wedding chant, tiring herself
With preparations for the nuptial feast.
At gaze, at play, or wandering, you'll find
Assisting her in everything she does
The long-haired Sojan, son of Chamir Shekh:

[1] In the Bengali edition Jasim Uddin notes 'Like gourd leaves her beauty is fresh and green, and as they soften in the sun she also softens with shyness, in blushes'.

[2] *Bell metal* is a white brass.

[3] A *puja* is a rhythmic prayer. This particular prayer has a light tripping metre and is used in a ceremony for warding off measles. It should be remembered that before the advent of medical science this disease was a killer. In *The Vision of Piers Plowman*, written in the late fourteenth century, our own poet Langland instances plague and measles as the two most dangerous diseases with which a man may be afflicted.

None knows so well what woods the civit cat
Has chosen for a lair to rear her young,
Or where the gullinule[1] has laid her eggs;
He'll shape a whistle from a mango seed,
Or laughing scale the highest branch to toss
Ripe plums into her outstretched eager hands;
Deft-fingered, he can fashion from the gab[2]
A wreath of rosy fruits, and thread a ring
Of bamboo stem to ornament the nose.
King of such lore, king to a maiden's mind.
Swirling like swallows of the riverside
They dance together through the village streets
With nupur bells[3] that tinkle as they stamp
To the tune of folk song and old nursery rhymes:

> 'Tomorrow is the jackal's[4] wedding day,
> Tag-dhuma-dhum, as they beat the big drum;
> He's walking now, a basket on his head,
> Towards the house of his father-in-law.'

> 'The house of Padmabati's[5] bridegroom lies
> Beyond the seven seas; yellows and blues
> Sift playfully against its gardened banks.'

> 'As I walked out to pick red cotton flowers
> In woods resounding with my shouts of joy

[1] The *gullinule* is a water bird.

[2] The *gab* is a fruit which looks like a small mango, green in its unripe state, vermilion when ripe.

[3] *Nupur bells* are worn on a ring round the ankle and are much used by dancers in India and Pakistan.

[4] The jackal is a very popular figure of fun and intrigue in Bengali folk tales, figuring in approximately the same role as the fox in our own folk-tales and fables. He may also stand for the half-europeanized native (a *babu*) who often plays a hilarious part in the literature of the sub-continent. It is natural, therefore, that he should coalesce with yet another object of humour, the prospective son-in-law. (Satyajit Ray's films have dealt with this.) A girl is often affianced, married even, at the age of ten or twelve, but continues to live with her parents until she comes of age. The bridegroom, meanwhile, visits his in-laws bringing presents to gain their favour; he is embarrassed, feels uncomfortable in his best clothes (which may include such an unfamiliar item as shoes) and has to be on his best behaviour.

[5] *Padmabati,* is a fairy-tale character.

I glimpsed a golden Champa[1] lady robed
In petals on a branch.'

No well-known maid,
This Champa, but the unsuspected friend
Of Kankabati[1] in the fairy tale;
And that's a secret only these two share.

[1] *Kankabati, Champa,* are fairy-tale characters. In addition the champa is
a yellow sweet-scented wild magnolia very common in Bengal.

CHAPTER 2

Though cows are brindled and of many hues
The colour of their milk's the same.
I wander through the world, but everywhere
I see one mother, many sons.

—Mendicant's Song.

When wise men become silent
It is because they have read
The palms of Christ
In the face of the Buddha.

—'The Search', Kwesi Brew. (*Ghana*)

There's no such tune as a black tune,
There's no such tune as a white tune.
There's only music brother,
And it's music we're going to sing
Where the rainbow ends.

—Richard Rive (S. Africa)

In Simul Toli village, where the trees
Shake out a breeze, the ground is cool with shade.
The Namu[1] and the Moslem houses stand
Beside each other, neck and neck; their thatch
Is smiled upon by the same sun and whipped
By the same gales. The Hindu quarter rings
With the sound of conch and gong on holidays;
Daughters-in-law and daughters fill the place
With cries of joy and laughter as they dress,
Gaily preparing for the festival.
When Moslems celebrate their festival
Of Id[2] both young and old are welcome there

---

[1] *Namu:* A member of the lowly Namasudra caste of the Hindus.
[2] *Id:* either of two Moslem festivals could be meant here, both lasting from three to four days. The most important is the great sacrificial feast when people

And the whole village joins the merriment.
Cocks crow and chickens cackle where they smash
Garlic and onion[1] fine; the curry's set
Upon the fire, and now and then a breeze
Carries its pungence to a Namu yard
Disturbing them no whit about their work.

The sound of drumming in Chaitra[2] turns
The village upside down; the Namus dance
And whirl about their posts, singing in praise
Of Siva.[3] All the people raise their arms
And join in chanting hymns. And if the noise
Should penetrate the mosque it is no cause
For quarrelling. But on the contrary,
Even a Moslem sometimes has been known
To sing some couplets at a Hindu feast,
And I have seen the lips of Moslems touch
The sweetmeats of the goddess Sharaswati.[4]

Untouchability's a burden few
Have bothered to sustain: the water blessed

wear their best clothes and go visiting each other, exchanging gifts; long visits, also, are made to the cemetery for prayer. The other festival is a time of rejoicing at the end of the Ramadan fast, a sort of equivalent of the Easter festivities after the long Lenten fast. Originally only a minor festival, it has now grown to major proportions.

[1] It is part of Hindu tradition that any member of the onion family (genus *Allium*) is unclean; as, also, are mushrooms. The fact that you often find these figuring in the dishes of the so-called 'Indian restaurants' may be explained by the majority of these being owned by Bengali Moslems.

[2] *Chaitra:* March 15th–April 15th. On the last day of this month the Chorok ceremony in honour of Shiva takes place. It is essentially a lower-caste festival, often characterized by the self-infliction of torture and, in this case, by swinging on or whirling round a post.

[3] *Siva* (or Shiva) is the most violent of the big three in the Hindu pantheon (the other two being Brahma and Vishnu), and is represented as world-destroyer as often as world-preserver.

[4] *Sharaswati* is the Hindu goddess of learning and eloquence. To maltreat a book in any way, however slight, is considered an insult to her. The point about the Moslems eating at her feast is not only that they are partaking in what to them is a heathen ceremony but, even more surprising, that Hindus are eating in their presence. To share a meal with a Moslem is unheard of. This is the point of the exchange between Duli and Sojan at the beginning of the meal in Chapter 13.

By the Preceptor[1] Namu mothers take
To sprinkle on their children when they're ill
Believing it a powerful remedy;
And by the Darga[2] Namu girls have kneeled
And bowed till the vermilion on their brow
Has stained a heart into the burning earth.

The tamarind[3] tree of the Namu house
Spreads its thin branches out to stray and sway
Above a Moslem yard; the mullah's[4] vine
Clings to a Namu's arbor whispering.
No one on either side protests at this,
For they are poor, their joys and sorrows small
And like, and all the village lives as one.
When her son dies the Moslem mother's grief
Flares in the candle of the Namu girl
Praying at night beneath the Tulsi[5] plant.
The sorrow of the widowed Namu's shared
By all the family and her Moslem friends,
When following the body to the pyre[6]
She breaks her bangles at its foot and smears
Away vermilion powder from her hair.
The sleeping pair within the grave, the pain
Which mounts in flames to heaven from the pyre,
Move still within the hearts of both alike,
Moslem and Namu mingled in one grief.

Where did they learn all this? I give my oath

[1] The Preceptor is a religious functionary among the Moslems. They too
have their sanctified water in the same way as Catholics.

[2] A *Darga* is a mosque erected round or adjacent to a saint's grave.

[3] The *tamarind* is a tropical tree belonging to the senna family; an infusion of
its seed-pods has a laxative effect.

[4] A *mullah* is the Moslem village priest.

[5] The *tulsi*, better known to us as basil, is a sacred plant which plays a great
part in Hindu death ceremonies. No Hindu yard is without a bush of it.

[6] Moslem and Namu death ceremonies differ in that the former bury their
dead, the latter burn them. After the rent-collector's murder in Chapter 17 he is
cut in half so that he may be disposed of both ways, thus indicating that it was a
joint operation and that his efforts to cause inter-religious strife would fail in the
end.

They never found one word or hint of it
In the Puranas[1] or in the Koran.
Not Arabic or Sanscrit taught this love
But the one sky that waves above their heads
It's blue enchantment, the one wind that wakes
Dark shadows in their woods, the equal rain
That knows no difference in them as it pours
In smoky billows sheer across their fields,
That moon upon its constant path that throws
Its ropes of light across the Moslem's fence
And freely strolls about the Namu's yard.

Greatest among the Namus is the name
Of Gadai; venerable alike his looks,
His port, his works, his place as village head.
His largest house towers up to touch the sky
And is prevented by a betel[2] tree
That throws its branches out to press it down.
Ten bulls are in his barn, four only pull
The plough; ten boys can hardly cope with them.

What better source of pride than his proud wife
Who certainly must be the avatar
Of Laksmi[3] come, mistakenly perhaps,
To bless his house. As stately as a barge
She moves from place to place, and woe betide
The miserable borrower of oil
Or salt she quarrels with; the very clash
Her anklets make expresses what she thinks
Of her unthrifty neighbours. I can swear
No father's son in the ten villages
Around is ever to be found so brave

[1] The *Puranas* are one division of the Hindu sacred books containing ancient
legends full of moral instruction. *The Koran*, of course, is the Moslem sacred
book containing the revelations (largely of a moral nature) given to Mohammed.

[2] The *betel* is the source of both nuts and leaves, very widely used for chewing
upon in the East; they have, eventually, a catastrophic effect on the teeth.

[3] *Laksmi* is the goddess of wealth and prosperity. An avatar is an incarnation of a god or goddess. Thus Rama and Krishna were avatars of Vishnu.

He'd dare to cross her in the slightest thing
Or lick the lime upon her betel leaf.
That water flowed by seven banks that fills
Her pitcher and the price of every grain
Of sand upon the nether region's floor
Is told upon her fingers year by year.

The bamboo cane of office in his hand,
Gadai is not afraid of anyone,
Gadai is proud enough to face the world.
But greater still the pride in which he holds
His only daughter, 'Duli', Dulali,[1]
For she it is who plays about the pond,
The vegetation matting its blind eye,
Who gathers flowers from bush and wood with friends,
About whose ankles tinkle oranments;
And she it is who spends her days in play,
Who dances at the head of all her dolls
To celebrate the first-fruits of the rice
Or else the marriage of the puppy-dog.
Sojan is always to be found by her,
Constant companion in her village rounds,
Egged on to play a hundred games or pranks.

[1] *Dulali* is the girl's full name; Duli, its contraction, is her familiar name;
cf. in English Kate from Catharine, and in Russian Katya from Yekatarina.

CHAPTER 3

The gang's off, are you coming fishing?
How can I with my foot all swollen
Unless upon a litter swinging,
Counting, counting, as I go
The six and eighty cowries there.

Pell-mell the water of this river
By the banks of sand that glitter;
On the moon-face the sun touches
The blood bursts falling.

> —Nursery rhyme.

Lavender's blue, dilly, dilly,
Lavender's green;
When I am king, dilly, dilly,
You will be queen.

> —Nursery song

The love of Sojan for the Namu girl
Is as the union of vine with tree
And tree with vine. If Sojan were the banks,
The river water swelling with the tide
In creaseless waves that pull against the sides
Is Dulali. Sojan[1] is truly named,
His nature tranquil and his works all good;
And though that river, breaker of its banks,
Rush wildly, it's the garland[2] round his neck.
He is the forest where his wild deer stalks,

[1] *Sojan's* name means, literally, a good person.

[2] Bank and garland are very common Bengali symbols. The bank represents security, the known. Flooding of the rivers during the monsoon is frequent; thus bank-breaking represents any catastrophe. Garlands stand for marriage: exchange of garlands used to be all that was required in the marriage ceremony amongst some castes. It will have been noted earlier in the vine and tree image that we have a variation on our own ivy imagery: 'just like the ivy, I'll cling to you', for example.

His leaves and vines spread out in nets of shade
To capture her; she knows the speech of woods
And haunts the secret tracts; she has no wish
To stray beyond the gentle bastions
Of greenery that fold about her days.

Such is the love of Dulali for him
That when she meets him on the path it seems
A coloured kite sails tugging at her hands;
And if he comes behind her calling out,
As if she pressed ripe mangoes to her lips
Or someone lifts her up so she can pick
Bunches of tumbling dates with both her hands.
Such is the love that flutters as the wings
Of the small nightingale which fans itself
Within its rose-bush nest, it seems to her
As if the tailor bird flew in her hair
And danced, and round her wrists red fire-flies flashed
For bracelets. Ah, if only she could shut
Him in her box of red vermilion, stretch
Her sari out, pulled to its greatest width,
To hide her Sojan there within its folds,
So that he never could be found again.

If Sojan does not come the day turns dark
On every side and Duli is as sad
As if her dolls were trodden underfoot.
When Sojan sickened once she rose at dawn
And vowed at Saving Kali's¹ door to give
An offering of seven buffalo
And to invite twelve Brahmins² to the feast;
She promised at the shrine of Jinda Pir³

¹ *Kali*, the mother goddess, is the female counterpart of Siva and is, in fact, his wife. Like him she is both saviour and, as in Chapter 6, destroyer.
² Brahmins are the highest caste among the Hindus. In the *Upanishads* (another branch of the scriptures) it is stated that merit may be obtained by making them gifts and feasting them. Since they are, in effect, the priestly caste, they are not supposed to take part in ordinary labours and, theoretically, must subsist on the offerings of the faithful.
³ *Jinda Pir*, literally 'the living saint', whose shrine is probably the Darga already mentioned. The practice of burning candles to him is yet another

To burn two hundred candles for his health.
Such was the joy she felt when he was well
She went about distributing to all
The date-stones she'd been hoarding, and her doll
With broken legs she threw to Puti, whom
She did not even like. Deep in her lake
Of happiness sank down the buffalo,
And Mother Kali did not mind at all;
The Brahmins were left hungry and the saint
Was dead so had to do without his price.
Besides, how could she leave her Sojan now?
It was unthinkable. She'd work to do
She'd never finish if he were not near.

She well remembers the one time he left
The village, though he promised to return
Within four days, when he went visiting
His uncle where the bamboo flutes are made.
And what a shopping list she gave him then!
He must procure for her eleven flutes,
And gather bundles of the quills that lie
About the woods, left by the porcupine.
There he will find the lotus-covered ponds
That sparkle in the sun like oystershell,
And see white herons circling round the woods
In search of the red berries for their food;
Deep in thick bushes where no-one suspects
He will discover hidden sugar cane,
Or else in rich profusion on the trees
Clusters of dates that scatter down all day.
Bearing all these, and more, he will return
And spend the day recounting all that's passed.

But Dulali had her commissions too:
That very day they'd seen with their own eyes
The new-born kittens of the civit cat

parallel practice of Moslem and Catholic. In fact some Hindu and Buddhist
writers, when speaking of other religions, make a distinction between Catholic
and Christian.

Romp in a field of swaying saffron flowers;
There she must go to pet them every day
And weave for them nose-rings of kolmi[1] flowers.
(Yes, what a joke!) On the red cotton tree
They'd tied an earthen pot and hoped some day
A bird would nest there. Let her watch for that.
Perhaps the tailor bird would lay its eggs
Upon the egg-plant. If it did, take care,
No one must know; eventually they'd find
Two tiny fledglings, one of which he'd catch
And tie onto her hair-braid so that it
Would flutter round her head. That would be fun!
And one thing more; the kittens in her house
Whose eyes might open after he had gone:
She must remember to save one for him
And no one else must have it; she must swear
By touching him, and he is satisfied

It's certain Sojan kept his promises;
Even among so many village folk
His equal is not easy to be found.
Who else can guide a coloured kite so well?
If need were he could fly, he says, with string
In hand, tossed high upon the wind into the sky
Where the glittering star-flowers are blossoming;
He'd sit upon the moon and weave those stars
Into a garland round about his throne,
And Duli, in the late hours of the night,
Could come and call to him, eyes red for sleep.
Suppose then he'd been born some flower or star,
Suppose he were the moon, not born a man;
If that were so it might suit him, not her,
For he could hardly recognize her there;
If so he'd better stay a farmer's son,
She's satisfied with him the way he is.
But just suppose her father should suggest
That she became his wife; that would not do,
Oh no, she'd die at the embarrassment.

[1] The *kolmi* is a creeping water-weed.

How much the story of his future life
Has been embroidered round this Namu girl.
When he is old enough, so old he can
Do anything he pleases when he wants,
Then he will trade in jute in distant lands
And cross canal and river to strange parts,
And when he had amassed a heap of coin
He promises he will come back and bring
A Madhumala[1] sari for his friend.

If you find peacock feathers there, buy some
For me, she says. And I should like to have
Caskets of vermilion, bangles of conch.
When he becomes a farmer he will plant
His fields with saffron flowers and cultivate
Them to his heart's content. One day the Spring
Will paint her sign across the earth and fill
With streaks of boiling colour places where
She'll spend her days slithering her feet through
        flowers.
He will destroy the jute for brilliant weeds
Whose beauty is outshined by Duli's smile;
And near the house he'll grow a pumpkin vine
For flowers, not fruit, to decorate her hair.

Now Madan's father is a grumpy man
Who scolds and curses anyone he finds
Has gone into his field to pick sweet peas.
He'll grow them for her and she'll come each day
To pick and pick until she has enough.

The sweet potatoes Sojan means to grow
Will far surpass the ones in Jamir's field;
He'll grow potatoes of such size as none
Have seen before. There's nothing he'd not do
To make her happy, spending all his life.

[1] *Madhumala* is a princess, heroine of a fairy tale. All saris have names which
indicate their design, the type of material or place of origin. The names of some
others are mentioned in Chapter 13.

CHAPTER 4

As the dew on the thorn that vanishes at noon
The man who has no caution says 'This body's mine'.
Castles of air you build, your waggon trails a star,
For at the hour of dawn the bird must fly.

—Murshida song

Between the idea
And the reality
Between the motion
And the act
Falls the Shadow.

—'The Hollow Men', T. S. Eliot

The sapla flowers[1] were smiling in the pond
And had not noticed that the drowsy moon
Was fading in its corner of the sky.
The swinging lantern of the morning star
Moved eastwards, and the charioteer of dawn
Had not unleashed his blood-red horses yet.
Dead fingers pick their way out of the graves
And ghosts creep stealthily into the homes
Where they slept once and now would wake no more.
Dead mothers standing at their children's door
Stare at them in the fire-fly light and fill
Their hungry eyes; remembering their love
Lost children kiss their mothers where they lie:
'In life-long grief you sleep, yet we are here,'
They weep. Tears well from the dead sister's eyes;
She lifts her baby brother on her lap
And thinks how they will never build again
Their playhouse in the courtyard of the world.

There is a sound of wailing from the paths
That run like ribbons past the distant fields

---

[1] *Sapla* flowers: a kind of water-lily.

Where swamp-lights sway; in the cremation plot
Devils and demons sob with the corpses.
The wind is whistling through the eyes of skulls
And every note in ten directions[1] shakes
The fevered darkness. On their stage of air
The Seven Sisters[2] dance an evil charm,
Their saris flapping down the Milky Way.
Fairy of darkness and fairy of sleep,
Creatures of dream, hoist up the palanquin
Upon their head and bear the sleeping prince
To Madhumala's shrine[3] with silent wings.

Then from the distance rose the muezzin's[4] call
And the still earth turned trembling to the sound;
The shrilling cry pierced upward to the sky,
And as a pond disturbed spreads ring by ring
The echoed note seemed pitched from height to height.
The vampire witch climbed up into the east
To spit out blood between her jagged teeth
And at her call the dead flew to their graves,
Devils and demons, muted, slunk away.
Upon the platter of the sky stars flared
And sank, the spent moon crumbled into ash.

And still the muezzin's cry of warning shrilled:
    'Beware, prepare, a fearful doom draws near;
    Oh you who sleep, O drowsy ones, awake,
    Put off the dress of sleep. Robbers have come
    And scour about your house, while with soft tread

---

[1] The ten directions in India comprise the four principal and four inter-mediate points of the compass, as well as upwards and downwards. It is, in other words, a three-dimensional system as opposed to the West's two dimensions.

[2] Seven Sisters: In Bengali this is the Apsari star-group of heavenly maidens who charm people, perhaps like the Greek Sirens. These I take to be the Pleiades.

[3] *Madhumala's shrine:* in the fairy-tale, Prince Madan is transported in his sleep to her ocean-island palace by two of the princess's attendants.

[4] The *muezzin* calls the Moslem faithful to prayer five times a day, if possible from the minaret of a mosque. In the morning he fulfils the function of the cock, or of an alarm-clock.

The expert burglar cuts into the wall
And steals into your sleeping hut to take
The necklace of white ivory you wear.'
Sojan awoke, and rising from his bed
Felt the faint stirrings, vague and imprecise,
Of guilt, but for what fault he did not know.
Beside his bed the bamboo flute had split;
A rat had come and gnawed the cowry sack
Loosing a heap of shells. He cursed the rat,
Scolded the flute, but neither understood;
His voice echoing, the only answer.

Seizing his flute he left for Duli's house
Along the winding many-coloured paths
Looking about with curiosity
To see the dates matured beneath dark leaves,
The swaying sugar-cane, and on a branch
The orange of new-ripened mangoes flash,
Ready to be unleashed by just one stone.
All this he'd show to Duli and the two
Of them would come to pluck and share the fruit,
He counting by mistake a smaller share
To tease her. A pure accident, of course!
Thus he delayed, looking at this and that,
At last arriving happy at the house.
        'Are you still sleeping, Duli? Come and hear.
        Lalu may go and gather all the dates
        While you lie there. And someone else might pick
        The copper-coloured mangoes from the tree
        For all you know. You better hurry down.'

Duli came running when she heard the news
But at the door her mother barred the way:
        'Where are you going? You're a big girl now.
        May seven vultures eat you, half-grown hag,
        You're much too old to play with young men now.
        What will the neighbours say, you cinder-face![1]

[1] 'Cinder-face,' and variations on this theme, represent the commonest
derogatory expressions of name-calling in Bengal.

How can I look them in the eye and hear
Them saying what a flirt my daughter is?
It's difficult to hold my head up high
Who owe not even lime to anyone,
What with your little games and flighty ways.'

What could she make of scolding such as this?
        She only laughed and said: 'Am I that old
        All of a sudden? Just draw near and look.
        I went and played with Sojan yesterday;
        If I was too old then you didn't say.
        How is it I've grown older overnight?
        I give it up. I haven't got the time
        To comb your hair for lice, I'm warning you.'
At this her mother swelled up like a frog,
Her anger crackled down from joint to joint
As she rained blows upon her daughter's back.

Sojan stood by resourceless and blank eyed
Regarding this injustice with dismay.
He walked away, foot dragging after foot,
Carless of where he went, blind to the path.
On either side wild creepers snared the way
And up above the trees' winged branches swept
The sky into their net. The little pigs
Ran off before him and the wild cats slunk
Into the undergrowth; young jackals raised
A cry that palpitated through the wood.
But Sojan walked alone down dusky paths
Where even at midday the crafty sun
Had never forced an entrance. Round his foot
A snake-skin wrapped itself and on his brow
Old cobwebs fluttered; weals and scars were etched
Like maps across his skin by bamboo bark.

At last amid a thicket ol bamboo
He stood upon the bank of the Rai pond,
Its inky water hidden under moss
And hyacinth, its ripples fettered fast

By kolmi creepers. Boars had churned the mud
On every side in quest of lily roots
And on the banks he saw the cobras' trails
Where they had come to drink and left on bark
And branch a shredded tatter of dead skin.
At dark the evil spirits come in groups
To light fires there and whistle through men's skulls
Disturbing the tranquillity of night.
A wife of the Rai family hanged herself
On that neem's[1] branch which still sags even now
As if to beckon someone else to death.

Idly he threw some stones into the pond
And shook a branch to watch the tearing mesh
Of lily petals float apart. Grown bored
He sat beside the neem outstaring space,
But what his thoughts were only he could say.

     Behind him jingled bracelets and two hands
     Were flung across his eyes: 'Guess who,' a voice
     Laughed at his ear. 'Could you be Haran's son
     From over there?' 'Says you,' the voice replied.
     'Ah, then you're Nabin's sister Batashi,
     I'm almost sure; or Ullashi perhaps.'
     'Drop dead at once, you silly cinder-mouth!'
     'Oh, oh, the pain, what demon fingers pinch
     My forehead so! Enough, I know you now,
     You're Bipin's uncle come back from the grave.
     Help, let me go, you'll be the death of me!'
     The giggling Duli took away her hands
     And stood aside. 'Such bravery,' she said.

'What a relief, it's only you,' he cried
With feigned surprise, but could not keep the smile
From breaking through his barricaded lips.
'Listen, my mother told me when you'd gone
How I must bear my age in mind and talk

---

[1] The *neem* or *margosa* is an Eastern tree yielding a bitter oil. Its leaves are used at funerals.

Accordingly, That meddling aunt of mine
And Khedi down the street have been at her.
I'd like to put a broom across their face
And stick a red-hot poker in their mouth,
The tattling busy-body cinder-heads.
How do they know we're old before we do?
I'd think we were the better judge of that.'
Shrugging his shoulders Sojan said: 'It beats
Me how we could have played so many days
Without age coming, and then suddenly
It's here without a word. I've never heard
Of such a thing before. It's very queer.'

> Dulali answered: 'Tell me, Sojan, what
> Is age? Where does it dwell? How does it come?'
> 'Don't you know that? It totters down the road,
> A palsied white-haired grandpa with a stick.'
> 'Then take a look and see if that old man
> Made a mistake and strayed into my hair.
> Tell me no lies.' Sojan undid her bun
> And scrutinized it to the very roots
> To see if that old man was wandering there.
> Duli became quite pale, he took so long,
> Afraid he'd say that age had come today,
> Had come to stay for good. At last he said:
> 'No, nowhere there, there's not a sign of him.'
> 'Then I shall go to mother straight away
> And ask her what she thinks she's on about.'

She rose as if to go but Sojan said:
'Need you rush off just now; why don't you stop
And play a while?' 'Speak bride, bo-katha-ko',
The bride-bird skimming through the tree-tops called,
Excited by the whistling of the boy
In imitation. Duli tried it too
But failed and asked him if he'd teach her how.
He pressed her lips together to a bow
But still she couldn't do it and she laughed
So much she thought her lips would split; she made

Sojan grow more upset with each mistake.
'You stupid girl, just put your tongue this way
And curl your lips a bit; now whistle so.'
When she succeeded Sojan was so glad
He danced and turned a cartwheel on the ground.
'If by tomorrow you've improved on that
I'll pick the blackest berries for your share
And make you seven nose-rings of bamboo
And give you a long necklace of kuch-seed.'[1]

  Dulali said: 'Your mouth is full of songs;
  Why don't you try to pour some into mine?
  I'll hold my breath and stand still open-lipped.'
But as he bent his face across to hers
Her mother crashed in fury down the path
To fuss and fume and bellow like a bull:
  'To think I've brought a witch up all these years.
  May snakes and tigers tear you limb from limb
  And ants crawl in and out, you wicked girl!
  And as for you, you little guttersnipe,
  I hope your father beats you black and blue;
  I'll tell him what a shameless brat he has.'

With slaps and blows she pummelled Duli's back
And pulling her behind she hurried home.
Sojan remained there struck as still as stone;
Where could you find the words to frame his thoughts?

---

[1] *Kuch seeds* are small and red, with one black spot on them. Goldsmiths use them as a small weight: 6 seeds = 1 anna; 96 seeds = 1 tola (rupee). In this they resemble carob seeds which were the ancient forerunners of the modern goldsmith's carat.

CHAPTER 5[1]

Kassem went forth to battle, woe is me,
A turban round his head;
The marriage bands were still upon his wrists,
The henna stains still fresh.
The Lady Sakina wept out aloud
For this sorrow, for this grief,
She'll never see him in this life again.

—Jari Dance Song

O lang, lang may the ladies sit
Wi their fans into their hand
Before they see Sir Patrick Spens
Come sailing to the strand.

[1] The story behind the Maharam festival described in this chapter needs to be told at length. Maharam is the first month of the Moslem year and the celebrations, among the Shiite branch of the religion, are held in memory of the massacre at Karbala in 680. The Shiites hold that the Caliphate should only be held by a direct descendant of the Prophet. In fact the only man to fulfil these conditions was the fourth Caliph, Ali (whose name appears in the Shiite battle-cry), assassinated in 661. Hereafter the split widened with tragic consequences. When Yezed (Ejid) became Caliph and held court in Damascus the faithful at Medina remained loyal to Hussain, the Prophet's grandson, and persuaded him to make a journey to Mesopotamia to rally his many adherents there. Hussain set out across the desert accompanied by his entire household and a small bodyguard but was cut off on the banks of the Euphrates by a large force sent by Yezed, who had heard of his design. After Hussain had refused to surrender, battle was joined between the vastly unequal forces and the men of Hussain's force, including their leader, cut down. Among these was the youthful Kassem who had only that day been betrothed to Sakina, and is said to have died in his uncle Hussain's arms. The news of this massacre and its victim shocked the Moslem world and did more to gather support for the Shiite cause than any effort of their somewhat ineffectual leader. A retaliatory force sent out from Medina engaged somewhat inconclusively with Yezed's forces. It was nothing like the revenge threatened in the present chapter. The Maharam festival, then, celebrates this melancholy event. Villagers sing and dance to Jari songs celebrating the battle, many examples of which appear both in the epigraphs and the text, and engage in sword-play with the very deadly canes used in the Bengali area. It is interesting to note the cultural synthesis which allows such Hindu manifestations as Kali's dance into the celebrations.

—'Ballad of Sir Patrick Spens'

Maharam, and the villagers have come,
Drunk with excitement, singing Jari songs,
To fence with canes. Today there are no poor,
There are no rich today, today for once
Wisdom and wealth cease to mean anything.
Great knowledge is the gift of Chamir Sheikh,
And he is welcome; Manir Miya is
A money crocodile,—this we'll forget.
(But Nayeb is the rent collector, so
He'd better stay at home; our tolerance,
Even on such a day as this, has bounds!)
Call the oil-presser Madan from his house
For Simul Toli's pride hangs on his cane;
Call Ram, bearer of palanquins, today,
Bindu the barber, Gadai, village head.
Let them all come prepared in battle dress
With canes and spears in hand, for at the shout
Of Chadan Miya peals of thunder split
The sky and from the sandy depths his cry
Of 'Hazrat Ali' echoes back again.

This day of days let us call Sojan out
To tell again Maharam's grievous tale.
There shall be no distinctions made, for chief
And follower are one where there is pride
In the brave heart and manly strength alone.
And we shall pay our homage at the feet
Of Boda-Ruddi, an oil-presser's son,
And show we've not forgotten, even now,
The story of the fight at Madanpur.
No longer can he wield his flashing cane
As in his days of youth; his eyes have sunk
Into their sockets, for one hundred years

58

Have passed him by, but still his skill of hand
And his courageous heart are no mere talk
In the ten villages around his home.
As Simul Toli's champion for years
His body bears a century of wounds,
Reminders of the battles he has won
To bear away the prize of victory;
Unbounded property and wealth untold
Would not be equal to such fame as this.

The boy of Simul Toli, if he wins
In the arena, finds his heart is full
Of many memories of the long past.
Surrounding him in a quick-stepping dance
We'll pull towards us in our net[1] of song
A tale of pity from Arabia.
But we must have Nitai the washerman,
The best of heroes though a poor man's son;
We cannot celebrate the festival
Without his wild inspiring presence here
Performing Kali's dance, broad blade in hand,
The thunder roaring from his throat to raise
A tempest in the river of our blood.

As players gather each direction's filled
With joyful clamour: Who has planted fields
With people surging like the rice in wind?
Who tumbled in confusion all the blare
And stir of seven markets on one spot?
Whose net has caught such crowds of milling heads?
Now through their midst the Jari dancing song
Plays like the ripples on a sea of tears
Telling the tragedy of Karbala.
Drawn on one side the village girls and wives,
And on another bands of children, sing;
Each answers each in gentle harmonies.

[1] The net is a very common image in an area so rich in fish-filled waterways as
Bengal.

Young men and old, Namu and Moslem, weep
To listen to the story of such grief.

Sojan is the new singer for today;
He dances, a red turban round his head,
Encircling the whole group, and tells the tale,
How Sakina was wife, and widowed maid
All in one day, the day of Karbala,
For when her husband's horse returned his corpse
Was laid across the back. The tide of grief
Burst open the black banks about her eyes
And channels of mascara coursed her cheeks.
She raised her wrists and broke the necklaces.
So newly wed, still in her marriage robes,
Is this the last she'll ever see of him?
And shall those hands that dressed him for the war
Prepare him for the grave on the same day?

Remembrance burns more fiercely than the sun;
There is no water that can quench its flames.
It was in vain she tried to rub away
The henna[1] dye that stained her hands and feet.
She tore her braided hair. Tear followed tear.
For very sorrow all the little goats
In her acacia woods kept close their mouths
And would not crop the grass. Her sorrow swayed
The hearts of Simul Toli and the waves
From far-off Karbala broke on its shore
With a soft murmuring that sobbed and sighed.
Still Sojan keened, his voice like a reed flute,
And Sahar-Banu's grief for her lost son
Was shared by every mother in the field.

Taking his comrades hands he ceased to sing,
He danced with whirling arms and bending neck
And with the dancing passed the days of pain.
Now he began the story of revenge,

[1] *Henna* dye is used as a cosmetic, especially at weddings, but is forbidden to widows.

Uncle and nephew's[1] vowed remorseless hate.
When Mamud Hanif heard of Karbala
The coiled-up cobra of his wrath was roused,
Swaying its hood as to a charmer's flute;
That news was like the trumpet to the horse
That lifts its neck and snuffs the smoky air,
His thoughts all ruin and his deeds all blood.
     'O Ejid, traitor's spawn, O cursed one,
     Would that I were a tiger now and had
     You in my hands. As lions seize a deer
     And snakes a rat I'd savage your soft throat,
     Break all your bones and rip you rib from rib.'

Beat with great pomp Medina's battle drums;
The yells of Mamud Hanif drown them all.
A thousand swords clang on a thousand shields.
Stout-hearted Jahar Ali grasps his spear
And brave Bir-Boksh is girded for the fight;
Like living cannons hissing into flame
Devouring all that lives in earth and sky
There Taleb Ali, Akkel Ali, march.
And Hanif rides about them with a shout
That thunders judgement like the day of God
To the confusion of their enemies,
For they shall pluck the earth up by its roots
And tear down heaven's pillars on their heads
Till all are smothered in that grave of wrath
Beneath the chaos of the universe.

Now is their hour and they will take revenge
For that cruel massacre at Karbala;
A thousand soldiers tread the doomsday dance,
A dance of fire as if a forest's breast
Were wreathed in flame and set alight the years,
Beating the heat into the human heart,
Burning in Simul Toli's men today
Till passions such as at the festival
Of flaming snakes inebriate their minds.

[1] The only male survivor of Karbala was Hussain's son; Hanif was his uncle.

From Sojan's throat it seems a cannon speaks
With words of shot; he tumbles, rushes, falls
And whirls with the destruction of that fire.
That trembling fire is dancing on all sides
And capering beyond horizon's edge;
Like flame there Sojan dances in their midst,
Molten his words, volcanic fire his voice.

Who loosed this avalanche of arms and legs
Stampeding like a herd of buffalo?
The villagers of Simul Toli whirl
Around in the wild tempo of that dance
Like spokes within a wheel that have no choice.
Madan is dancing with his flashing blade
As if he'd split the world up like a log;
Here prancing Gadai twirls his bamboo cane,
There Madan Miya makes his dagger dance.
Nitai the washerman in Kali's place
Shrivels the heart-strings with her stricken yells;
As if the seven oceans of blood
Were in her maw, heaven and earth are scarred,
And finger clawed on finger raised to weals.
Madness is in her laugh; fainting she falls
And rises in her frantic dance to raise
Such clamours that the sun is put to flight
And riven skies are quivering with dread;
She wails, she beats her breast, her woman's heart
Is loaded with a grief too great to bear.
It is as if some robber snatched away
Her only child and now her weeping eyes
Water the paths by which she goes in search
Of him; but she will have revenge, revenge
Will fall on him who bares a mother's breast.
Hate fills the room up of her stolen son,
No tiger that has lost her whelps so fierce.
So dances wrathful Kali on that field.

The dance ends and the fencing games begin;
Pairs are assembled, young men matched with young,

Elder with elder, boys with boys. Today
The brave will demonstrate their bravery,
The skilful show their skill and charm the crowd
With intricate and rhythmic play of canes.
Dolu's an expert hand, but dancing's all
Chadan can manage; Rohim must sit out
The game because he does not know the rules.
Look, Madan Miya has aroused himself
And plays as skilfully as he can dance;
You cannot find his equal far and wide.
Will Jaga play with him! There, with one twirl
His guard is broken and his head is struck.

> Then Sojan said: 'Although I cannot hope
> To win I'd like to match myself with you.'
> Madan replied: 'Come on, the pleasure's mine;
> I'll show you a technique to beat all skills.
> Give back this thrust. Bravo, you're doing fine.'

The two began their play, whirling their sticks
In circles as the potter spins his wheel,
As lightning roars through clouds to strike the trees,
Or as one kite swoops on another kite,
The mongoose plays the snake, hawk fights with hawk.
Three skills[1] were passed and Sojan shook his stick
And took a stance, ready to start the fourth,
When Madan whirled and struck a mighty blow
Which Sojan dodged, snatching away the cane.

> Madan cried out: 'Well done, young man, the fame
> Of Simul Toli rests secure in you,
> I'm proud to say. This cane of Bhalk bamboo
> Passed down to me two generations old;
> I've spent my life defending its good name.
> A murderer from Kajan Danga fell
> Before it and at Talma fair it helped
> Defeat the Ban Ga villagers.
> For thirty years I've brought along that cane

[1] The cane game follows a predefined procedure, the skills representing
different ways of handling the cane.

You've won so cleverly to celebrate
This festival. The village's prestige
Hangs on its point. No one until today
Has ever beaten me and I had thought
It would be mine until that day the earth
Is piled above my grave and it will lie,
Once highly prized, neglected in the dust.
Now it is yours, and if I had my wish
I'd dance you on my shoulders to the bounds
Of earth and up into the sky above.
This cane was fashioned from the good bamboo
Of Simul Toli and for its defence;
See that the boundaries are never changed,
The fields are safe, while it is in your hand.'

Just then some trivial dispute occurred,
The Namus and the Moslems bickering,
And soon a crowd was drawn like flies to meat.
The quarrel broadened like a forest fire.
As pots of water will not quench its rage,
As useless are attempts to stop it now;
It only will intensify the more
And turn soft words to fuel for its fierce heat.
Saud-para's Khans nursed long a bitter grudge
Against the village folk and now they had
The Namus there revenge was in their grasp.
The Sheiks of Bhajanpur threw in their hand
With the aggressors and the fray began
With clamour, clash of sword and cane, with cries.

Imagine at a Moslem festival
How few the Namus were and how they fought
In that unequal match with desperate might;
Small wonder they were beaten in the end,
Outnumbered thus, for all their bravery.
Retiring, some with shattered wrists and some
With broken legs, they vowed undying hate
For such as dared to raise their hand and strike
The hoods of the Hindu cobras in this way.

CHAPTER 6

Pair betel nuts with betel leaves;
Flies and mosquitoes must be caught;
   Bring these.

—Drug Charm

Winnowing fan and broom in either hand,
Half of the body black, the other red,
The goddess rides upon the tiger's back
And seeks whom she'll devour. Woe to that man
That dares to stand in Vengeful Kali's path.

—Charm for Smallpox

We know who it is that has said 'Vengeance is mine,
I will repay'; and again, 'The Lord will judge his
people'. It is a terrible thing to fall into the hands
of the living God.

—Hebrews 10:30–1

Ram Nagar's agent Nayeb,[1] publican
And sinner, heathen, scoffer, heretic,
The very devil, death personified:
How else would you describe the poor man's scourge
Who calculates whose rent is in arrears
And auctions off the house about his ears?
With salutation fees, bribes for default
In paying rent, burdenous interest,
Poll tax, excesses and deficiencies,
His dewlap and his money bags are filled;
Layer on layer, day by day, his fat

[1] Nayeb is a representative of the old, bad, social order in Bengal where all the land belonged to a landlord (zamindar or jamidar) and the poor peasant worked it for him, as in Europe's feudal system. The rent-collector is his agent, collecting both rent and taxes and taking his cut, often using extortionate and generally Rachmanite tactics. In this way he often resembles the tax-farmers under the old Roman system (although they bought the right to collect taxes and then had to make a profit), the hated 'publican (and sinner)' of the Bible.

And his demands grow mountainous and more.
When he puts out his hand a money tree
Scatters its golden fruit into his palm;
His every movement is a clink of coin,
His conversation hiss and whispering,
Huddling in corners, becks and nods and winks,
Sly as a pig with an acorn to hide.

So small a thing that pen behind his ear,
And yet its story's not so innocent;
We're only too aware of that pen's power,
See it unvarnishedly and know its work.
The hand that wields that pen can fell a town:
One stroke and all the houses lose their thatch,
The hearths are left deserted, weeds break through.
The pen writes on, a village turns a grave,
But who dares ask for news of those that sleep?
The pen wipes the vermilion from the brow
And widows pull their husbands to the pyre.
Dabir of Gajan Tali went to jail
For seven years, a victim to that pen,
And Kalutila's Namu quarter burned
At midnight, sacrificed at that pen's will.

Gods do not stir beyond their temple walls,
At festivals are satisfied with gifts
Of flowers and the leaves of the passion fruit;
And peaceful Allah does not leave the mosque,
Content with prayers and offerings for the poor,
And the fasting ordained at Ramadan.
If we neglect our duties He stays there,
And hungry gods call no one to explain.
But Nayeb's not like Allah or a god;
His altar is the spot on which he stands.
A law unto himself, he prowls around
Demanding his own terms from whom he will:
Land rent, arrears, trust money and a bribe;
The man that will not pay has burned his boats,
Puts nails in his own coffin, bells the cat.

A writ, a writ, whoever takes no heed
The doves will circle his deserted home,
Rats rule the roost, and insects play the host.
A writ, a writ, seize the bell-metal cups,
Snatch up the pots and pans, tear from her nose
The housewife's ring and kick her in the face.
A writ, a writ, for those who ride the storm,
Who fight in equal contest with the floods
And dwell on shifting sandbanks with no fear,
For those ferocious tigers dare not face
Who in deep jungles build their villages,
For those who dance in frenzy with the ghosts,
Witches and demons round the Shaora[1]
At the wheel festival, and do not flinch,
For those who draw the poison from the snake,
Even for such as those, a writ, a writ.
Who dares pronounce these spells on cobras' hoods,
What weather charmer's horn blows through the hail
To pacify the tempest with his breath,
Whose magic stops the demons in their tracks?

A writ, a writ, no clothing and no food,
The hungry baby cries, but rent is paid.
Rent, he wants rent, Nayeb the yellow cur;
The little girl can die for want of milk,
Her mother hang herself with her last rags,
For all he cares—so long as he's paid rent.
A writ, a writ, the landlord's son will soon
Get married and his agent will not give
Receipts unless you pay an anna more
On each rupee. His daughter celebrates
The first rice ceremony,[2] writ, a writ:
Eight annas extra on the rent receipt.
No wriggling out of it; cough up and grin;
That man would dun his father if he could.

[1] The Shaora tree figures in yet another of the wild and whirling dances of
the elemental Siva worship.
[2] The first-rice ceremony celebrates the first solid food a baby eats after it is
weaned, about six months after its birth.

Our crops have just been ruined by a flood,
Our houses buried under water, cattle drowned;
Who cares about the landlord's son at times
Like this, what has his marriage got to do
With us? Who's interested? Oh what's the use!
Look, here we go again: A writ. A writ.
So round and round the wheel of fortune whirls
And with it cringing bows and jingling coin;
The rent collector holds it in his hands
And like a god controls the life of men.

Quite late one night as Nayeb sat alone
With law suits turning over in his mind
A shuffling and a scuffling at the door
Brought him to earth. His eager visitors
Jostled and pushed to bow down at his feet:
The Namu band, Nitai the washerman,
Gadai, the barber Bindu, fifty more.
Never was night as dark as were his thoughts:
        Allied these Moslem curs and humble castes
        Are getting swollen-headed nowadays;
        They think the world's a drinking cup for them.
        The landlords want their village as the site
        For a new market and it's up to me
        To get them out. I've got the writ all right,
        The law is on my side, but if I were
        To let it out, just in so many words,
        They'd get above themselves and answer back:
        'Oh Mr Nayeb, sir, where shall we go?'
        Am I the servant of their grandfather?
        Where can these honourable gentlemen
        Betake themselves? As if I cared! Am I
        My brother's keeper? Anywhere they like,
        Into the jungles, through the wilderness.
        That's all about it; I know what I know,
        And Simul Toli's the new market-place.
        But look how brave they are, how they neglect
        The landlord's order, laugh and joke and move
        About the streets as if they did not care.

They're laughing up their sleeves at me; they'll laugh
The other side their faces when I'm through.
He laughs the longest who laughs last, that's sure.
I'll show them, though, go to the civil court
And bring a writ against them, then the laugh's
On them; let's see if they can smile at that.
But wait, suppose those Namu bastards join
Their mangy Moslem friends and they show fight,
Then that would really set the fat on fire.
I'd better watch my step or anything
Could happen; nothing must be left to chance.
It's no use touching pitch to be defiled.'
He knows what he's about: playing with fire,
Once burnt, twice shy; he's playing games with snakes,
Once bitten and you get no second chance.
Deceit and craft are woven in the net
He seeks to cast about the innocent.

Puff on the hubble-bubble, cough a bit
And smile a bit: 'Ah, Gadai, village head,
What can I do for you? Come closer, tell
Me all the news; what have you got to say?'
Saluting him again with folded hands
As if to take the dust of Nayeb's feet:
'Oh, sir, my heart breaks when I think of it;
At the Maharam fair the Moslems joined
Against us in a fight and beat us so
We barely got away with our own lives.'

The rent-collector roused himself in rage,
Like a banana frond his body shook:
        What's that you say; are Moslem dogs that brave
        They dare to strike the heads of Namus now?
        And after cutting off the cobra's tail
        Can they sleep peacefully in bed at nights?
        Have rats rebelled and pulled the kitten's fur?
        What turn of fortune makes the fishbone stick
        In the porpoise's throat? Can this be true?'

'What could we do,' asked Gadai, swallowing,
'When seven villages of Moslems joined
Together in a band and leapt on us?
They frightened us and caught us off our guard,
Or we'd have shown the louts a thing or two.
But we have come to ask for your advice;
In your opinion, what should we do now?'

Nayeb replied to him in angry tones:
        'Is it my place to tell you what to do?
        Is Gadai headman to a band of ants?
        What do you think your cane is for, you fool?
        Has Nitai left the village to its fate
        And let the yellow rust eat up his spear?
        Has Bindu, Madhu's son, abandoned you?
        Where is the big scythe of the boatman, Gaur,
        Where is the axe of woodman Dukhi Ram?
        Can Kanai Ram no longer find the range
        With his harpoon, is it no longer sharp?'
        'We are all here and wait for your command;
        There is no hope for us without your help.'

Enraged, or so it seemed, Nayeb jumped up:
'I'll give you orders; wait a moment here.'
His eyes were flickering like catherine wheels
When he returned, vermilion on his brow,
From praying in the temple; in his hands
He carried garlands of red Jaba flowers
That seemed to drip hot blood from their torn mouths.
He thundered, 'Now I'll give you a command,
And all who come to me tonight shall wear
A wreath in token of obedience.'
Gadai the headman answered him with pride,
And all assented: 'Yes, whatever fire
May burn on it, we will all wear that wreath.'

        'You'll wear it then, you'll wear it on your neck?'
        Demanded Nayeb loudly, burning-eyed,
        His pyrotechnic voice crackling with sparks;

'You'll wear it then, you'll wear it round your neck,
This wreath of Vengeful Kali's Jaba Rose,[1]
Red as the blood of heads torn off by her.
Wearing this wreath come running like the bands
Of rain and hail from the wind-king's whirling swing;
Come like the demons and the witches, come
As Kali flies to the cremation ground,
Violent Kali chapleted with skulls,
And set alight a torch of fiery snakes.'
Thus saying Nayeb garlanded each neck
For Kali's worship, but with tongue in cheek,
An unbelieving hypocrite at heart.

All bowed and said, 'We wait for your command;
What must we do wreathed thus?' Nayeb replied,
'At midnight break the Moslem quarter up
And drive them from your village while it's dark.
Behead with the long sacrificial knife
The Moslem dog that hinders you in this,
And thus pay back the insult of the fair.'

Nitai the washerman cried out aloud:
        'Nayeb, I bow to you down at your feet;
        Take back the wreaths and let us go back home.
        Ten villages of Moslems did this thing;
        On what pretence must we turn on our own?
        Indeed, they fought for us, fell back with us,
        Were beaten the same way; how can we take
        Revenge on friends and drive them from their homes?'

Nayeb burst out in rage, 'The reason why
You Namus never quit your humble caste
Is that you have no pride. If you had sense
You wouldn't brook a currish Moslem's blows.
One Moslem or another, it's the same;

---

[1] The *rokta* (bloody) *jaba*, better known to us as the China rose, is not actually a rose but a member of the hibiscus or mallow family. To this family also belongs that plant from which are gathered the edible pods known as ladies fingers, *okra* or *bindhi*. The jaba figures in sacrificial garlands sacred to Kali in her terrible aspect.

The body suffers when the head is hit
And every member trembles with the hurt.
You cannot pass this up, for if today
You let yourselves be beaten at the fair
Tomorrow it will be the market-place,
Next day and ever after in the fields,
Or on the path, and everywhere you work.'

    'I think I can explain it,' Gadai said;
    'I sadden at the thought of beating them
    Although I know that we outnumber them.
    If we attacked we'd get the upper hand,
    But it would be as if our canes were turned
    Upon ourselves because we have so much
    In common, houses side by side beneath
    One grove, and over it a single sky;
    Scorched by the sun or drenched in rain we pull
    Our ploughs in the one field and share the times
    Of happiness and sorrow like good friends.
    Have pity, Nayeb sir, take back your wreaths
    And your command, and call us what you will
    So long as we remain, as now, at peace.'

The rent-collector gave his anger vent,
His scolding scorched like fire: 'Out of my sight,
You bastard tanners,[1] lowest of the low!
Since you will not obey I'll get a writ
To pull your houses down and seize your goods;
I'll confiscate your land and dig in posts
Of good bamboo to the official drum.[2]
If I don't break you Nayeb's not my name.'
Bindu the barber clasped the ranter's feet
Imploring, 'Sir, have you no other wish
That we could carry out instead of this?'
'No I have not!' his shouting pierced the sky,

[1] For a Hindu to be called this is a deadly insult. The killing of animals in order to tan the hides is considered ritually unclean. Only out-castes and Moslems perform this work.

[2] Bamboo posts and drum: the official procedure when land is seized or claimed by a new owner.

'This night that Moslem quarter must be sacked.'
'Then be it as you will,' the Namus cried;
'Since we have come so far, let us go on
Whatever happens; there's no turning back.'
'Bravo,' said Nayeb, 'now you're talking sense.
Like loyal devotees you must obey
Blood-thirsty Kali's orders.—On your way!'

The moonless night was surging with black waves
Lit only by the flickering of ghosts
Parading the canals with eldritch lamps.
Owls screeched about the woods where deeper still
The breast of darkness settled on the trees.

CHAPTER 7

Immure yourself behind great bolted doors,
Construct huge bastions:
Yet you yourself will die, my friend,
And do you weep for that?

—Murshida Song

Here forest fires are flaring, there
The highland's carpeted with nets;
Hunters advance with bows bent back,
With jaws extended pythons wait.
What can the fawn do, or where flee,
When fate pursues him thus?

from Vidyakara's *Sanskrit Anthology*

No more the farmer's news, the barber's tale,
No more the woodman's ballad shall prevail;
No more the smith his dusky brow shall clear,
Relax his ponderous strength, and learn to hear;
The host himself no longer shall be found
Careful to see the mantling bliss go round,
Nor the coy maid, half willing to be prest,
Shall kiss the cup to pass it to the rest.

'The Deserted Village', Oliver Goldsmith

Night turns to dawn. At Simul Toli's mosque
The Moslems gather, hardly knowing why.
A copper lamp that swings from side to side
Surveys their faces, calculating thoughts
Too apprehensive to be put in words.
About the moonless sky the plunderers
Of light, the stealthy stars, shield shattered beams.
In fitful gusts a cool indifferent wind
Twists though the crackling leaves as if it were
Some restless wake-a-bed that tossed and turned.

Among those gathering such quiet reigns
The lighted lamp is led to meditate
Silence's silver beauty. In the graves
Around the mosque the dead all recollect
The story of their lives, retelling them
To the still night upon whose breast the lamp,
Attentive always, listening to their tales,
Inscribes them with calligraphy of gold.

Cautiously, voices hardly audible,
The people come and go with silent steps,
Belongings wrapped in bundles on their backs
And sleeping children carried in their arms.
They hurry from their houses to the mosque,
Their anxious faces hidden by the dark,
And speak in signs so that no sound is heard.

Then from far off the muczzin's mournful call
Straining to pierce the tangle of the dark
Welled up and ebbed into the dusky paths
Bringing the last few stragglers to the group.
Before them stood the mullah, eighty years
Of wrinkles hidden in his full white beard.
With peaceful face he read them the Koran
In senile tones that quaked as if the woe
Of the whole world were pouring from his throat.
On Judgement Day the Prophet of the poor
Will clasp the throne and thus shall wake such tears,
Bringing to mind the sorrows of this life.
Such weeping trembled in the reader's voice
That the whole realm of nature, every beast
And bird, each tree and leaf and vine, were joined
In grief with him. The keening of his chant
Was like lamenting Majnun as he lay
Alone on Laila's grave at dead of night;[1]

[1] The story of Majnun and Laila, one of the most popular in the Arab world
and an equivalent of our Romeo and Juliet, is one of several keys to this work in
which coming events cast their shadows before them. It is the subject also of
numerous Persian and Moghul miniatures. Unfortunately there are many
variants of the story. Basically it is the story of the poor scholar Majnun's love

His wasting candle's flame was like the grief
Consuming him, and the thin drops that fell
From it accompanied his bitter tears.
So Munshi Saheb read, and reading wept;
Grief followed grief as words poured from his throat.

> Closing the book at last he said: 'My friends,
> This village has no further place for us
> And this is the last time we'll gather here;
> All must be left behind, both house and field.
> In our last moments let us pray to Him
> Who rules the universe . . .'. Just then there rose
> Chamir the fencer, lathi-stick in hand:
> 'I'd like to speak, sir, if I may. I know
> Your knowledge is superior to mine,
> Of course, but fail to see your reasoning
> In this advice. While we have canes shall we
> Be driven from our village? If we left
> In craven fear how could we hold our heads
> Up high, a byword and a scorn to all?
> Let come what may, we shall defend our home,
> Our father's hearth, though Azrael[1] should fight

for the rich and beautiful Arabian girl Laila. Several factors seem to hold them apart. Family differences in one version; a Persian miniature shows an engagement between their rival clans. In other versions it is a religious difference; a Moghul miniature shows Majnun seated like an ascetic in half-lotus position and dressed like Gandhi. Added to this some say Majnun was incredibly ugly and Laila would have nothing to do with him, yet a Persian miniature shows the two fainting upon first meeting each other (and one assumes this is from love and wonder). A Persian story in the *Gulistan* tells how a prince visited Majnun and asked him why he was so despondent; upon hearing glowing praises of the beauty of Laila he rushed off to see her himself and came back disappointed and reasoning that beauty was in the eye of the beholder. At any rate Majnun's frustrated love drove him raving into the wilderness where his father came to visit and reason with him; men hid behind rocks and peeped with pity and terror, while does gazed at him from thickets, their soft eyes big with wonder. Somehow love triumphed eventually and Majnun returned only to have Laila die on their wedding day; he, of course, died of grief shortly afterwards.

[1] Azrael is the angel of death, holding roughly the same position as Hermes, the Greek guide to the Underworld. Quite a sociable chap if he had no business with you at the time, and willing to stop for a chat. He actually visits Solomon to pass the time of day, according to a story in Rumi's *Masnair*, cf. Burn's 'Death and Dr Hornbook' and the Button Moulder in Ibsen's *Peer Gynt*.

Against us; why, cling to the very soil
Rather than let a stranger take our place!
What is your answer, comrades? Speak today
And show your bravery. Shall we stay here
And fight like men or skulk away like thieves?'
All rose and dinned, 'We'll never run away.
Fighting, there is perhaps a chance to live;
If not, we'll fill the village with our graves.'

Then Sojan rose and spoke, beating his chest:
   'Let he who wishes go, but as for me
I'd rather dash my breast against the stone,
I'd rather fall in battle, than do that.
Hundreds of days with freight of joy and woe
Have come and gone beneath our houses' thatch.
The swaying trees have spread a fan to cool
Our village as a mother does her child.
The earth has given up her golden crop,
Her breast received the wounding of our ploughs;
Here we have laid to rest beneath the soil
Our fathers and our brothers, and made wet
The arid dust with sorrowing and tears.
Our love is mingled in the soil of graves
And every particle of dust is dear
To us in Simul Toli. If today
We're cowardly enough to quit this place
Our fathers and great-grandfathers will rise
And curse us from their graves. Five times a day
We pray inside this mosque, obedient
To prophet and Koran, and following
The paths of God. To whom, then, shall we leave
The mosque if we should leave? We'd never hear
Again the muezzin's sunrise call to prayer.
You who have placed your people in the graves
Beneath their flowering bushes, make a group
And pray for them to enter Paradise,
For if we leave them thus and sneak away
We'll have to answer to them on the day
Of Judgement in the meadow of God's court.

Can you tell me a purer place to die,
A better reason to give up your life?
For if we die, here shall our graves remain
To make a holy Mecca of this spot.
This village is my home; I will not leave
And not defend its soil. If life is lost
The losing is more precious than to gain
Life without point, for he who seeks to save
His life can only lose what makes that life
Worth living, friends, and home, and self-respect.
To die with honour is to live indeed.'

In tones of tenderness, with slow smooth voice,
    Old Manir Munshi spoke: 'My friends, I know
    That you are listening to your heart's blood sing,
    Letting emotions overmaster you.
    Though I am old, in the sea of my breast
    A tempest blows as well, and it is good
    To let the swaying joys and sorrows raise
    Such waves. But hear me first; then you may judge.
    Ram Nagar's agent, Nayeb, has enraged
    The Namu men with subtle stratagems,
    For they are ignorant and have not learned
    To know yet who are friends, who enemies.
    As you have heard, the Namu band has joined
    Three other villages at Bangor's field
    And even now are sharpening their spears
    And dressing up for war. Now we are few,
    Too few to turn the fury of their charge
    When they advance. I do not doubt at all
    Your readiness to die; but ask yourselves,
    Who will care for your children when you're gone.
    Allah does not inhabit clay-built mosques;
    Why should we bring destruction on ourselves
    For a few bricks? Wherever Moslems live
    A mosque springs up, but if the men are dead
    How shall the mosque be built, who will there be
    To worship Allah? Speak, my friends, who will
    Defend the honour of a pile of bricks?

Why should you Moslems leap towards your death?
Now listen to my plan. We'll hasten off
To Kaji village and our brethren there
Will shelter us. Our numbers will be great,
And if needs be occasion may arise
To take revenge for this in equal fight.'

His words were like sweet butter to them all,
Dropping with softness, sympathy, and love.
All gave assent to follow his advice
And flee to distant Kaji from all harm.

Then Munshi Saheb raised his hands in prayer:
    'Oh, Allah, kind and great, you who survey
    The whole world from above and keep account
    Of all the good and bad in every life,
    Your will be done. Now in this night of grief
    Befriend us, show your sympathy with us.
    We leave, entrusting to your care the trees
    And vines of Simul Toli, and we ask
    Your blessing on the fruits and flowers they bear.
    The fields are ripe for harvest and their skirts
    Are rich with jute and rice, yet we, her sons,
    Must now desert this yeasty mothering earth,
    Filled with affection for her though we are.
    This love engraved upon our memories
    Will always last, however far we go.
    We suffer now the cruel flames of grief,
    And yet determination to return
    Will beat upon our pulses day by day.
    Each atom of our being will cry out
    In every waking moment to go home
    And weep for Simul Toli in our dreams.
    For all who stay behind asleep in graves,
    Our forefathers, we'll take a last salaam.'
And with these words he slowly left the mosque
And stood before the graves in silent grief;
The people followed, overcome by tears,
To pay their last respects before the dead.

Head bent, hands raised to heaven, deeply moved,
     The mullah prayed, 'Oh, God, Lord of the poor,
     Our forebears stay behind enclosed in earth;
     Let blessings rain upon them night and day.
     Listen, you dead, our final prayer's for you,
     We'll no more gather by your graves like this,
     On nights of mourning light our candles here,
     Nor will the fragrant incense fan the breeze.
     Lord of the universe, all-seeing One,
     Fulfil our last desire and bless these dead.'

Then Munshi Saheb opened the Koran
To read them words of comfort in their grief.
At length he walked away, pace after pace
With wistful slowness, loth to leave the place,
Across the fields, through dim and misty night.
Still he repeated verses from the book,
Scattered their pain to the horizon's rim;
The weeping people followed in his steps
Bowed down by all the sorrows of the world.

CHAPTER 8

The wild swan flies away,
His shadow falls behind:
A man returns
To his own land,
And who'll stand in his way?

—Murshida Song

Yet let me flap this bug with gilded wings,
This painted child of dirt that stinks and stings.

—'Satire on Codrus', Alexander Pope

The Namus, for their part, were weaving nets
Of argument in Bangor's field. All night
They'd spent at bending bows and hurling spears.
They had not fought for many a day and rust
Had gnawed their weapons, weevils bored their canes,
Inroads of rats had holed their battle-dress.
The very thought of battle fired the youths.
Impatiently they fretted restless limbs;
Courage leapt high as a hind to the heart.
Hand grappling hand and chest opposed to chest,
They leapt and twirled their swords; gong-metal clanged,
The war-drums beat, pulsating to their shouts.
Now they had weapons reason would not hold
Their hand till they had proved their worth.
Gripping their spears and arrows, stamping earth,
They rocked the firmament with their fierce cries.

With gloomy thoughts the old men sat apart
Unable to decide what they should do.
Nitai broke out, 'It's no use arguing.
There's no returning; let us carry on.'
But Gadai said, 'My mind agrees with you
And yet my heart's unwilling to assent.

Can you forget that those we mean to strike
Today are kinsmen in a way? I ask
In all humility, can we destroy
Those houses which we helped to thatch and ran
To drench with water when they caught on fire?'
'I know just how you feel, chief,' Nitai said,
And clasped his hand, 'but what we can't get round
Is that we've Kali's orders to obey;
We'd have to face the rent-collector's eyes
Of copper-coloured wrath on top of that,
So I'm afraid there's nothing we can do.'
'Let's get it over with,' the headman called,
'Come on, my friends, there's no retreating now.'

Mad with enthusiasm the wild band
Of Namus blew their torches to a blaze,
Flailing a thousand blades with savage shouts.
They march, they march; the grass of Bangor's field
Is trampled underfoot, the naked fire
Dances along their arms from sooty flares.
Like roaring waves that thunder round the seas,
Like sheets of lightning leaping through the skies,
With Siva's trident balanced in their hands,
They march and will not spare whatever men
Or demons cross their path to victory.

Behind them Gadai shouted for a halt:
        'Brothers, we must turn back; what good will come
        From killing neighbours of another faith?'
        A thousand Namus cried, 'We won't turn back
        And never will. Today we'll weigh our lives
        Upon the mighty balances of death.
        Who hears the urgent call let him advance;
        May he who falters in the path be crushed
        Beneath a victor's foot. Let cymbals clash
        For battle and strike up a hymn of death.'
        Past the cremation ground, past mosque, past wharf,
        They march, they march to Simul Toli's ford.

The headman strode in front to block their way:
      'Stand back or let my life-blood quench your thirst.'
They stumbled to a sudden huddled halt,
      And Gadai called, 'Whom do you march to fight?
      What lands of dazzling conquest blind your eyes?
      Have you forgotten Sojan, among men
      A man whose rising puts to flight the ghosts,
      Brings fear and trembling on the Evil Ones?
      Remember now the day of our dispute
      For water rights against the villagers
      Of Bhat; whose cane was raised in our defence,
      Who felled the foe and won canal and pond,
      Who led the Namu band? You may be sure
      Ram Nagar's puppet *babu* wasn't he,
      That dandy Nayeb, gentleman of ease.
      Much more his line these orders to prostrate
      Our village till it's weak as a wet cat.
      Who was it taught us how to hold our canes
      But those whom we propose to turn against
      With so much bounce, and beat at their own game?
      By whose advice are we to do this thing?
      Nayeb's, of course—the same one who recoils
      If we so much as look as him, he who
      Withdraws across the street and scorns our touch.[1]
      You'd think it was an honour he allows
      Us when we are permitted to bow down
      And hear him call us bastards, sons of dogs.
      Is it for him, who hates the Namu caste,
      That we must drive the Moslems from their homes?
      They sweat with us beneath Chaitra suns,
      Their hands are calloused by the plough like ours;
      In danger or in hardship, storm or shine,
      They are the ones who come when we cry out.'

      But Nitai said, 'I dare not disobey
      The order of the goddess; I'm afraid
      To go back home and anger her this way.'

[1] Nayeb scorns their touch because, since he is of a higher caste, it would render him ritually unclean.

'Can you be sure that this was Kali's wish?
Might not this be some higher god's command
Before whose shrine the jackals crouch, where cats
And dogs have leave to come and go unharmed
But Namus stray into disaster there?
Oh no, this isn't Saving Kali's work;
I know what I'm about, I understand
At last. We have the words of him who thrives
From sucking out the life-blood of the poor,
Who drives the weakest to the wall, and grinds
His face into the dust. Consider, now,
If Kali would be likely to command
Such things; we've only Nayeb's word for it.
He is the one who auctions hearth and home,
Who drives us from our houses with a kick.
Advice like this can only be from him.
Shame on us all to trust the likes of him,
To wear these wreaths as if we worshipped him!
We should have flung them from us hours ago;
Tear them off now, shred out and crush the flowers
And trample them. Get rid of this disgrace.'

Gadai was trembling with a fearsome ire,
His eyes expressing feelings such as none
Had ever seen before. They tore the wreaths
From round their necks and strewed them in the road.
Before the eastern gate of dawn there stood
The goddess Kali with dishevelled hair,
Blood flowing from her mouth. Wailing she clutched
The far horizon, stamping underfoot
The shards of darkness, the last shreds of night.

CHAPTER 9

Though you unloose the knot of love
The fires of separation do not die.

—Lyric Fragment

Remembrance wakes with all her busy train,
Swells at my breast, and turns the past to pain.

—'The Deserted Village', Oliver Goldsmith

Stars lead the morning in, true to their vows,
    To tread in letters of red lac[1]
On Namu courtyards with their ricepaste tints[2]
    The smiling messages of dawn.

The water gurgles to the white lake's brim
    Among the large and smaller hithes.
The bustling maidens murmur quietly
    The holy verses and the vows
Propitious for the winter rice in Magh.[3]

Girls bend to sip[4] from broken reeds and greet
    Slim flower-maidens rising up
From that strange land beyond the rushy brink;
    And where they bathe the water leaps
In peacock sprays to lash the other bank.
    The mistress of the garden sits

[1] Red lac (*alta*), a cosmetic used for painting the soles of the feet.

[2] Ricepaste tints (*alpona*): Rice kernels are soaked in water until soft, then mixed with vermilion powder, turmeric, or some other colouring matter and used as a dry paint for making designs in the dust of the courtyard.

[3] *Magh*, January 15th–February 15th. It is common to plant two or even three crops of rice a year. Such intensive farming, of course, impoverishes the soil even in so potentially rich a province as Bengal. It explains why famine is becoming so frequent in that area.

[4] Sipping water through reeds is a common way of drinking in Bengal.

Alone and smiles to see the play of waves
    In subaquatic flower-pavilions.
An offering of marigolds is borne
    Beneath the surface in its tray;
The colours swirl and blend, gold with the blue.
    Flowers load the bushes with their freight,
Boughs bend beneath the multifoliate
    And garden-filling mass of bloom;
Untouched upon the foremost grow the buds
    The gardener forbids his wife.

Verse after verse, the children's hubbub grows
    And fills the pond from side to side.
Tattling in groups the gathered village wives
    Gossip of this, gossip of that.
Altars for measles puja are prepared
    With bundles of wild durba grass
And flowers in every yard; while on all sides,
    Now bowing and now standing straight
Reciting scriptures, stand the girls and boys.
    The mango-jackfruit altars brim
And overflow with sacrificial ghee,[1]
    And over them the older men
Beat drums to call the Brahmin to the house
    And give away their daughters.
Chirrup of children's voices, verses, vows,
    Fills all the street from Namu yards.

And then it was they brought the mournful news
    Of how the Moslems had all left.
Numb-handed worshippers let fall their flowers;
    Abandoning upon the banks
Their half-filled pitchers wife and maiden ran,
    Their tear-streaked saris at their eyes,
To search each house and cottage for their friends.
    As always, there the buildings stood,

---

[1] *Ghee* is clarified butter obtained chiefly from the buffalo and prepared by
melting the originally solid butter, cooling it slightly and pouring off the
liquid portion, which constitutes the viscous ghee.

But their inhabitants had gone, and who
        Knows where or why. No worshippers
Were at the holy shrine; each cat and dog
        Could wander unmolested there.
The empty mosque where at the hour of dawn
        The Moslems stood for their last prayers
Housed only oxen now that stamped the floor
        And gouged their horns into the wall.
The grinding stone is left neglected, half
        The turmeric uncrushed; where did
The grinder go? Picked only yesterday
        These henna leaves remain prepared
And no one here to crush them underfoot.
        That compact left upon the ground,
Has Sakina let fall her wedding gift?
        Look, fluttering from branch to branch
Of the red cotton tree friend Madina's
        Tame pigeon cries for her in vain.
The east wind blows in Maynamati's yard
        And tosses to and fro red herbs
That reach their tendrils for the mullah's house.
        Whom do they signal, those dumb hands,
What do they spell with their bright semaphore?

        From house to empty house they go,
Women bemused in their simplicity,
        And find no comfort for their tears,
No reason for desertion such as this.
        And who can tell what Duli feels,
Ashamed to weep, unable to suppress
        The sorrow stirring in her breast
That must express itself but finds no way
        Save in wild laughing now and then,
Aimless, hysterical, and unexplained.

Events succeed each other like a dust
        That settles on the past, each day
Another film that covers up old cares.
        And yet there is a Namu girl

Whose heart grieves constantly, and who will not
      Admit to it, or say for whom,
Except in solitary colloquy:
      'Alas, you runaway, was there
Not time to bid goodbye and shed a tear?
      Did haste stop up your thoughts, and did
It not occur to you how slow the days
      Would pass for one you left behind?
Had you no single moment you could spare
      For one who has too many hours
Of weary loneliness now you have gone?'

      Now Duli must live out again
In memory all of those treasured days
      She passed in vanished happiness.
Beautiful dreams like coloured bubbles come
      And go upon the mind's lithe swing
And burst into the air without a trace.
      How had they come? Where had they gone?
Awake, asleep, they drift about her mind
      And pluck their poignant scale of grief
Across the fretted vina[1] of her soul.
      And she remembered now that time
They'd quarrelled over nothing as they played
      And she had said, 'I'll never speak
To you again, not even if I die.'
      Then Sojan climbed to the cat's lair,
The highest branch of the tamarind tree,
      And threatened, 'If you do not speak
To me immediately I'll jump down right
      From here.' How soon she broke her vow!
Then they had sat together at the foot
      Imagining they flew like birds
Across the sky with bright-hued flashing wings.

[1] The *vina* is a plaintive stringed instrument of the stick-zither family with a
resonating calabash at either end and several movable frets, as in the Japan-
ese *koto*. It is played with one calabash resting over the left shoulder. There
are five principal wire strings played with a finger-plectron and one or two
outriding steel strings tuned an octave higher and played with the little finger or
thumb.

How was it possible he'd had
It in his heart, that Sojan, thus to leave
        Her so, and what was there to keep
Him far from her this way? But when he went
        He had not even one last word
To say, that was the hardest blow of all.
        Unhappy Duli, left with this,
Her utmost grief, to rankle at her heart.

        She has another memory,
The sorry incident of the Rai pond
        When they had tried to imitate
The whistling bride-bird and her mother came
        And beat her back so that it left
Great whorls and swelling weals, and it was sore
        For days. Had he forgotten that,
How she'd endured such torture for his sake?
        The rumours that the women spread
Were worse to face than all her mother's wrath;
        They'd cackled on for weeks and weeks.
Now what was left of it but a sore heart
        That knew no ease, a grief untold,
Sorrow that irked and aggravated more?

        It was the heavier to bear
Because she had no friend whom she could trust
        With such a precious confidence.
Only at dead of night from forest depths
        The flute of someone swells and dies
Repeatedly. Whoever plays that flute
        On some far path in the late hours
And scatters secret sorrow through the leaves
        In his unearthly tones, could he,
Perhaps, know of the weeping in her heart
        And be acquainted with her mind
Whose own seems full of suchlike tears and sighs?

CHAPTER IO

Have I deceived myself thus far
By keeping close my grief?
I can no longer stay in lands
Where I find none to love.
          —Song of Separation

Let's go far away from here,
Let's follow any path,
. . . . the path of dreams.
Behind us someone said,
'Dreams have no paths.'
      —*Pequenos Canciones*, Fernando Garcia Bravo

The Namu nuptial songs reverberate
    Upon the wind; filling the air
The women's ululations,[1] drum and conch,
    Resound together, rend the sky.
Today the legend is enacted once
    Again, and Rama shall be joined
To golden Sita as in those old days
    When first he bent great Siva's bow
And won his bride; types of the faithful pair,
    As Vishnu's other avatar,
The husbandly ideal, Krishna the dark,
    Whose consort Radha, skilled in love,
The memory of whom a thousand lives
    Were not enough to dispossess,
Was such a mate as all men hope to gain.
    Unfolding down the centuries
Heroic histories repeat themselves,
    And every village gallant might

[1] The word ululations stems from the Ancient Greeks who, like Indian and Pakistani women of today, made an 'ulu' sound at times of great emotion. I suppose it resembles the old Red Indian war cry, much beloved of children and Tarzan fans today, made by emitting a high-pitched 'ooo' and slapping the mouth with the hand.

Be Ram come back, Krishna descended once
      Again to lead his people or
To war with demons and thus save the world.

The bridegroom's mother has no time to spare;
      Will she be finished when the bride
Is welcomed in; oh where, where shall she find
      The ceremonial durba grass?[1]

      'Where is the golden peacock, the sun's friend?
      Along the sky-paths he is flying.
      Oh swoop down, bird, fetch me the durba grass
      That in Malini's[2] garden overflows.'

With tender voice the village girls give back
      The very echo of her thoughts
Upon the waves of song. How many times
      Have humble Sitas gone to meet
Their Rama in the distant house of guests![3]
      Some cook, some put the final touch
To marriage decorations, all work hard.
      In Gadai's house it seems the din
Is fit to shake each rafter in the roof.

Who are those two young people in the wood,
      Whispering together, veiled from sight?
With such festivities upon all minds
      No one would think to notice them,
And yet it's strange on such a day as this.
      'Sojan, my marriage is today;
Just look, I've bathed in turmeric, my skin's
      Translucent black now glows with gold.
Vermilion on my brow, red lac my feet,

---

[1] *Durba* grass is used in the welcoming ceremony at weddings.
[2] Malini is mistress of the garden and wife of Mali the gardener. (There seems to be an allusion to them at the beginning of Chapter 9.) This is an extract from the traditional wedding songs which friends of the bride gather to sing on the wedding day.
[3] A guest house is specially built to serve for such ceremonial occasions as weddings.

My body dressed in finery,
Bracelets of conch, a sari of red silk:
    Why should I summon you today?
Draw near, I'll whisper it into your ear.
    Dressed even so I'll run away
As far as eye can see and feet can flee
    If only you will take me with you.'[1]

'What's this I hear, you silly little girl;
    Can't you distinguish good from bad?
Bring up a child to know the way of right;
    She will not leave it when she grows.'

'The tender branches of bamboo will curve
    In the direction they are bent.
I only know that none from childhood up
    Have understood me as you do.
When we were young you promised many times
    We'd always face life side by side.
We are two flowers out of a single bud
    And someone else now threatens one.
Will you not pluck her first, does not your heart
    Say anything, counsel this course?
You've not much time to think; already night
    Is mingling the wood-path with dusk.
Take both my hands and pull me down the path
    With all your strength for even now
The Namus are out searching in high rage.
    Before they come we'll cross the wood
And swim the Kumar. On the other bank
    The path across the field of flax
Is thickly strewn with leaves. That we will take.

[1] Duli's action here is especially momentous. There is no stigma attached to a
Moslem marrying a Hindu in the democratic Moslem community. But a
Hindu renders himself (or herself) untouchable or worse by such an action.
In the most rigid Hindu system no one can become a Hindu except by birth
into a Hindu family, although some groups, as the followers of such reform
movements as Radhakrishna's, do allow converts among them. It should be
mentioned, however, that this is not so hard-headed as it sounds since the
Hindus believe in reincarnation. If you want to become a Hindu sincerely
enough then you will probably be born one in your next life.

Where there's no tell-tale dust and none
Can follow in our tracks to drag us back.'

'Alas, you're still as stupid and your thoughts
      Stop short beyond that forest path.
When will you wake up to the consequence
      Of such an act? Some evil hour,
Tomorrow or today, we will be caught.
      Perhaps it has not crossed your mind
What's to become of us? Grant that I take
      You with me and we disappear;
Your wicked-tempered band of Namus will
      Attack my village in revenge
And tear the place to pieces like wild beasts.
      And who's to help the helpless then?
No, no, you must go back. Bite off my head,
      Do what you like, my little girl,
But if you love me follow my advice.'

'Sojan, you're only thinking of yourself;
      What will become of where you live,
Your brothers and your friends? Just like a man!
      Have you considered me at all?
If this is how things stand then why did you
      Spin those beguiling stories when
We were both young, visions like paper-chains
      And intricate designs in bead
Stringing our lives together without end,
      Visions delightful any way
You looked, that side and this, above, below,
      Caught in the breeze and streaming out.
How I admired you then, and now I can't
      Conceive of life apart from you.
And do you bid me take my leave of you
      For good and all? I cannot go.
You were the tree, I the enclosing vine;
      Your branches were a cooling breeze.
Can you now banish me to a strange land,
      To strangers' hands, strangers for kin?

From childhood all your stories thronged my ear,
    Repeated morning, noon, and night,
And now bear flower and ripen into fruit
    So that my soul enmeshes yours.
Oh Sojan, Sojan, how can I forget?
    A human being's not a stone!
Stones smash into a thousand pieces, grind
    To dust, and does a soul do that?
The lips incarnadined with betel juice
    Can be light-heartedly wiped clean;
Your words are henna-stains upon my heart,
    Burnished to brilliance when they're scrubbed.
You do not understand this helpless girl,
    You can't see further than your nose;
How do you think she's going to pass her life
    With strangers ignorant of her?
The heart is not a slab of cake you cut
    And give a little slice to all.
How can I give another what I gave
    To you, alas, and only you?
Oh, can't you help me, tell me what to do?'

'I know, I know, the memory persists
    To rub salt daily in your wounds.
All I can ask, I make no other plea,
    Is that you'll try to bear the pain.
I'll always hope and pray with all my heart
    That blessed day is not far off
When you'll be able to forget this time.
    It wasn't far from here we joined
Together newly planted banyan sprouts,[1]
    One male, one female, mine and yours.
The new leaves clasped each other in the breeze,
    And every evening we would come

---

[1] The banyan tree, a relative of the mulberry, has branches which send out
aerial roots, thus forming additional stems. It is the Indian fig-tree under
which the native shades, mentioned by Milton in *Paradise Lost*. By planting the
two banyans side by side Sojan and Duli were symbolically marrying the trees
whose branches and stems would interpenetrate, rather like the linked chestnut
arbours you sometimes see in formal English gardens.

With pitchers filled to tend and water them.
     Their branches flourished with our love
And we would say that just as we had wed
     Them trunk to trunk so our two lives
Would be forever joined, branches entwined.
     Today we have outgrown our games,
We have no further need of these twin trees,
     So let's uproot them now in case
They should remind us of our childish tales
     And stir old griefs in days to come.
Here's where we joined together Kadam branch
     And Mango bough and sat beneath
Debating which was bridegroom, which was bride.
     And when the Mango branch had flowered
We took all day to wed the Kadam[1] tree
     To her with ceremonial pomp.
The rainy season came and wreathed that tree
     With smiling flowers; then with glad songs
The Mango tree was given this new bride.
     When you approached your sari trailed
With rippling colours on a petalled lawn.
     We promised if some day our paths
Should lead divergent ways we'd cling as tight
     To one another as we'd bound
These trees. Now if we should unloose their bonds
     Today our compact too would break;
So let us cut their ties and end these tales
     Never again to be recalled.'

'Oh Sojan, wait! Before you break the ties
     Which bind these plants so laughingly
Construct a vine-noose, hang it from that tree,
     Lift me and put it round my neck.
Tomorrow when my parents ask for news
     Of me tell them some savage beast
Devoured me in the forest depths. The hand

[1] The *kadam* is a flowering tree associated with the love-play of Radha and
Krishna. From its flowers are made the wreaths which bride and groom exchange at the wedding ceremony.

With which you root the banyans up
On which we lavished so much childish care,
    That very hand must guide the knife
Into the channel of my throat and let
    The blood spurt through its broken bank,
Impounded once but unimpeded now.
    And when the villagers inquire
Say I was bitten by some poisonous snake.
    Report my boat of life capsized
Beneath a shoreless sea where I lie drowned
    Deep as a vanished continent.'

'Unhappy girl, rocked in titanic waves,
    Withered by oceanic irons,
I scarcely recognize the child I knew,
    The Duli that I played with once,
She's learned to say so many things today.
    Alas, why did I loose this flower,
This slender girl, to float on sorrow's stream?[1]
    The rice-chaff flame,[2] I knew, would scorch
My soul with such incineration as
    Ravana's ever-burning pyre.[3]
I thought that only I would feel such pain,
    Bearing all torture in my heart,
But now those flames have caught your sari's end
    And kindled you into a blaze;
Alas, unlucky girl, there's no escape
    And you must suffer all your life.
But I alone am guilty of your pain;
    Try and forgive me if you can.
You shall be witness at the Judgement Day[4]
    How cheerfully I'll wrap around

---

[1] Setting a flower to float aimlessly down a stream is a standard image in Bengali love poetry.

[2] A rice-chaff flame is particularly hot and another frequent image.

[3] Ravana is a demon with ten heads and twenty arms who was, in some accounts, specially punished on an ever-burning fire for daring to make war on the gods. Later mythology makes him a firm devotee and favourite of Siva.

[4] The Judgement Day (already mentioned in Chapter 7) is as much a part of Moslem eschatology as it is of the Christian's.

Myself the fiery dress of Hell and hug
        The cruel flames so that no part
Of me escapes its withering embrace.

        Today you must forgive and go;
I did not realize your fresh green vine
        Wrapped round my sick and puny tree
Could be so blighted and its blossoms die.
        If only I could be assured
That when I go my back alone would bear
        The consequences and the grief
Of my mistakes, and no one else need share.
        There! Did you hear that distant cry?
That's bound to be the Namus on their way.
        We can't afford to linger here;
You must be off before they spy us out.'

'Oh, there you go again; how typical!
        No one would mind if you were seen,
But think what they will say when they find me,
        A girl who runs into the woods
Upon her marriage day. You are a man,
        All paths are open to your feet,
All ways and all directions safe for you.
        But mountains hem a woman in
On every side if she should leave the path.
        Go if you will; I have no power
To stop you. Leave me with the heavy weight
        Of scandal dogging all my steps.
Go if you will, you're welcome, but I'll leave
        You one last thought to take away.
You've stripped my life of flowers and left me thorns.
        And when the Namus come and find
Their vanished bride, think of the price I'll pay.
        Out of the scandal I have caused
They'll weave such shocking stories from today
        That I shall suffer all my life.
They'll prick like spear-grass any way I lie:
        I'll toss, I'll turn, but still they'll goad,

Spare me no rest whether I stand or sit.
        Well, all right, go; yes, off you go;
I'll add this fiery portion to my shame.

        Bear off the blossoms from my tree
Of happiness; I know that you'll forgive
        If on the surface of your moon,
Over the tranquil ocean of your sky,
        My scandalous intrusion casts
Its shadow briefly. What's my life to you!
        But you're absolved from blame, of course;
I'll take my punishment and go in peace.
        From this day on you must forget
That anyone named Duli ever lived.
        No need to worry any more,
I blundered on your life then spun away
        Like a burnt moth. Like water weed[1]
That straggles in the current then floats free
        I touched upon your river bank.
We pass like boats at night and go our ways.
        Laughter abounds where there is life,
And in its midst this tale will slip your mind,
        This light-weight load on childish hearts,
These acts of simple silly innocence.
        Now that we part for the last time
I bow and take the dust[2] before your feet.
        Give me your blessing that this dust
Might fortify me through a thousand griefs.
        Be witness sun and moon with all
Your starry train; be witness righteous gods
        And all the forest trees and leaves,
Now and hereafter none shall have my love
        But Sojan, captain of my soul,
Sojan, heart's husband, more than mind to me.

[1] Water-weed adrift on the current is an ever-returning image in this poem
and in the popular lyric. It is usually associated with a special type of song, the
bhatiali or ebb-tide song, dealing with separation and frustrated love.

[2] Taking the dust signifies the traditional Indian gesture of greeting and
departure and is a sign of humility: it is that of holding the hands outwards,
palms together, as if in prayer, and lifting them to the bowed forehead.

Mother and Father witness this,
Be witness friends and brothers, kith and kin;
        Marriage vermilion witness this,
Be witness you conch bangles on my wrist,[1]
        How I've received the cruelest hurt
Of all my life today at Sojan's hands.'

'All right, come back then, Duli, and we'll run
        Wherever feet and fortune guide.
If you insist on ruining your life
        No one can override your whim.
But have you thought what hardships lie in wait
        If you persist in this design?
On every path the thorns will pierce your feet;
        Under the burning suns of noon
The golden creepers of your limbs will wilt;
        For lack of food your tender lips
Will droop beneath a sigh and split on words.
        You'll sleep at night on beds of leaves
And from the overhanging jungle vines
        Black pythons slither by your head;
Tigers will slink nearby with fearsome yells.
        Bushes of thorny cane will catch
Your clothes and scratches gouge your silken skin;
        You'll stumble, clutched to ribbons, cut
So often trickling blood flows ceaselessly.
        Then it will be too late to turn;
Whoever takes the first step on that path
        Continues for a thousand miles.
Your name will come to mean reproach and shame;
        The parents that you love will turn
More alien than your worst enemies
        And your familiar friends will hunt
Remorselessly to tear you limb from limb.
        Then there will be no hiding-place.

[1] Wrist bangles are worn only by married women. It is for this reason that
Sakina breaks hers in the Jari song quoted in Chapter 5. The vermilion spot
on the forehead and sprinkled in the hair-parting are other signs of the married
state.

Much as you fear snake's stealth and tiger's tread
        More terrible will be the dread
Of parents' wrath. There's no returning then
        To that old carefree village life,
But skulking with the animals at night
        And hiding from the light of day.
Think carefully; you still have time to leave.
        Why throw yourself upon the pyre
Before your gleaming sun has risen high;
        Why waste before they have begun
The wealthy days that glitter in your path?
        The mistakes of a moment must
Be paid for by a lifetime spent in tears;
        Decisions seal our destinies
And then not piety or wit can lure
        Back time to cancel half a line
Nor all your tears blot out the fate decreed.'

'Don't think I've not deeply considered this.
        But my whole world is where you are
And I'm a stranger when you are not there.
        What do I care, if I'm with you?
When bands of beasts are baying in the wood
        I'll hold my peace, locked in your arms;
And when my weary stumbling body tires
        I'll look into your handsome face
And feel a moon-like courage rise in me.
        On rainy days along the way
I'll spread my hair and make a little tent
        Where you can lie while I reach out
And deck it with the wild flowers from the wood.
        When we are hungry you can climb
The highest trees and gather heaps of fruit.
        When feet are bruised and travel-sore
From walking in the jungle I will break
        Your weariness with childhood tales;
We'll face the world again, refreshed with song.
        I'll go wherever you will lead
And give my darling all the stored-up love

I've had for him since first we met.
We'll build a happy nest like tailor birds
        That perch up high so gingerly.
But listen; now the hunt is drawing near
        And there's no time for further talk.
Let us become two shadows in the wood
        And melt into the cowling night.'

'Allah be witness, prophets witness this,
        Saints and preceptors witness how
I'm taking this unlucky girl tonight
        Down the paths that are perilous.
Be witness sun and moon with all your stars
        Now we are homeless in the night.
Be witness throne of God and Holy Book
        Now we have left our homes for good.
People of Simul Toli, neighbours, friends,
        All kin and family, witness this,
For none of you shall see us two again
        Now that we take a random path
And follow where it leads, bidding farewell
        To childhood here. Let no one speak
Sojan and Duli's name from this day forth.'

CHAPTER II

Devils and demons, where will you run, now
That Siva links dread hand with Parvati?
They dance with all the Himalayan heights,
The bangles jingling in their matted hair;
Harrow of steel they are, and iron plough.
Chandi the fierce declaims, 'I'll break the neck
Of all I catch and suck their marrows dry.
And if my charm should fail let Hara's head
Spin from the neck and roll upon the ground.'

—Hail Charm[1]

In peace there's nothing so becomes a man
As modest stillness and humility,
But when the blast of war blows in our ears
Then imitate the action of the tiger,
Stiffen the sinews, summon up the blood,
Disguise fair nature with hard-favoured rage.

—*Henry V*, William Shakespeare

What happened then, what happened? Suddenly
   The Namu marriage drums have stopped.
A great commotion fills the village streets,
   Swells loud, swells louder, louder still.
What happened then, what happened? Search the paths,
   The hythes, the forest and the fields;
Search everywhere, by the cremation ground,
   By Baghar's barn . . . who is it runs

[1] *Hail charm:* I suppose this is meant to hold off hail by invoking Siva's terrible whirling dance, calling up winds and rain. In this his matted hair is wound round by a snake from which hangs a chaplet of freshly severed heads, the movement of which looses the Ganges from his locks down to the ground. In this terrible aspect the name Hara (seizer) is applied to him. He is joined by his wife, here called Parvati (of the mountains), daughter of the Himalayas, and also known in her terrible aspect as Chandi (the fierce). The iconography of Siva during this dance is said to resemble that of the ancient pre-Aryan shamans or wizards.

So swiftly underneath the banyan trees?
        What happened then, what happened? Stir
The marsh-grass on the waters of Rai pond.

        This way and that the Namus go
And push aside the lotus with both hands.
        Thick darkness mantles every side
But 'There they go now, look!' shatters its midst;
        Now here, now there, and then far off,
Vanished like smoke. Then 'There they go now, look!'
        Through mustard-planted marshy land,
Across, beyond the field of Gajani,
        Sword-sticks and torches in all hands,
The angry Namus overtake the wind.

        Leaving the shelter of the canes
A little to the left, 'Look, there they go!'
        Crunching of leaves beneath the feet,
Hordes of dark figures fan into the chase.
        They're going down by Bangor's marsh,
It's clear to see and 'There they go now, look!'
        Come running, run, swing stick, swing sword;
Cut all the vines and creepers to one side
        To look for footprints, off you go.
They are escaping with the Namus' pride;
        He who has power must snatch it back.
The one who treads upon the hood of snakes
        Must have a panther's bravery
And be the tiger's cousin if he thinks
        He does it with impunity.

The Namu honour soars beyond the sky
        When such a slight is cast on it
And they must have revenge at any cost
        Wherever he may flee or hide.
They'll rip the heavens open with their spears
        And bring him plunging down to them.
Though he should beg the mountains fall on him

The rocks would grant no hiding-place.
Though he should lurk in Hell they'd dig him out,
    And if he changed into a fish
Then they'd be dolphins scouring through the sea,
    If scattered small as mustard seed
They'd be the pigeons pecking clean the ground,
    Or should he melt into the wind
As lightning they would circle him with fire,
    And if he mingled with the sea
They'd be the storm that drives the churning waves
    Till they had found and brought him back.

What happened then, what happened? On a branch
    A red silk wedding sari hangs,
And silver anklets in the linseed wood
    Are found abandoned by the path.
Out-distancing the wind the hunt pursues
    With whirling swords, sharp-pointed spears.
What happened then, what happened? Alta stains
    Have brushed the surface as they passed.
Press on, slash through the jungle, keep eyes skinned,
    And search, keep searching, search and search,
Scour on till the horizon meets the sky.
    Night passes, gentle day has dawned,
And still they circle through the weary glades.

What happened then, what happened? 'Nayeb, sir,
    A blow has fallen on our heads,
We men of slender means. Our honour's stained
    By one who has escaped our homes
And taken to the woods. Earth's pillars shake,
    And mountains topple to the ground
When our clean cloth is smirched with spreading shame.
    A marriage bride has run away,
And we don't know what unbeliever's hand
    Has dared to perpetrate this crime.'

'What news from Kaji village have you heard?'
    'Sojan was missing yesterday

And people saw him in our neighbourhood.'
    'Now that's exactly as I thought.
Take up your canes and swords, shout for the kill,
    And with that battle-cry strike out;
The winds will wilt, the nether regions burst,
    The sky come tumbling down like wax.
Set fire to all their houses, burn their fields,
    And put the people to the sword
If they oppose your search. Then there's the jail
    And district police for later on;
I'll take responsibility for that
    And issue a decree, a writ
To auction off what's left of heath and hearth.
    I'm on your side, you needn't fear,
And I'll so twist the law I give my oath
    Those Moslems shall depart in tears
And flee from path to path without a home.'

CHAPTER 12

Amir, his courage rising, bound
His war shield tightly to his back
And armed with Hazrat Ali's sword
Strode forth to battle for revenge.

About his waist the dagger's sheath,
A golden turban wound his head;
He held a blade in either hand
And angrily he roared 'Strike home!'

—Jari Song

O delicate walker, babbler, dialectician Fire,
O enemy and image of ourselves,
Did we not on those mornings after the All Clear,
When you were looting shops in elemental joy
And singing as you swarmed up city block and spire,
Echo your thoughts in ours? 'Destroy! Destroy!'

—'Brother Fire', Louis MacNeice

At Kaji village, in the mullah's house,
Great preparations have been made for days
And now the Malud Sharif gathering
For teaching and for prayer is close at hand.
No one can sleep a wink for worrying
Who to invite and whom they must exclude
From all the seven villages around.
If they invite the villagers of Bhat
The ones who live in Khapur will be vexed;
What would they do, and how could they explain
If those from Mural Daho were left out?
There's Bhajan Danga's Kajir-Pora and
There's Tepakhola's Achel Khara house,
And all the Mirdhas from up Komlapur.
Whichever way you look the number grows.

By nightfall Saturday the mullah's yard
Is overflowing with the happy crowd.
Who recognizes whom in all this crush?
Foremost of all, mascara case in hand,
Is Madan Kulu, come from pressing oil
All day. Who minds if Nidan Fakir is
A hired man only? Equal with the best
He takes flower-perfume from the mullah's hand.
Son of a bearer, Kalimadi shines
So no one seeing him tonight would think
His occupation covers him with dirt.
And who would guess that Ali-mammud digs
Thigh-deep in mud all day seeing him wear
His handsome jama[1] and new finery?
Bright-coloured bend and sway of fez on all
So dazzles you'd imagine Paradise
Had scattered flowers to earth from every gate.
Who waves his golden wand above this house
So that the very village seems to glow?

Now who'd believe the people of this place
Would strike a blow in wrath or fill the jail
For lynching or assault and battery?
They're only stiff-tongued farmers, like wild beasts;
Their scolding shows affection and their rage
Is vented on the slashing tips of canes.
You wouldn't think it now to look at them;
It's just an outer husk they cast away.
Emerging colourful as snakes that slough
Their skins they gather peacefully tonight
And sit together in their Sunday-best.

It is as if someone returned from pilgrimage
Has spread his date-frond prayer-mat souvenirs
All through the bustling courtyard, glad with pride.
Stretching above them is a canopy

---

[1] A *Jama* (it is the same word as appears in 'pyjama') is not a piece of night
attire but applies to a long coat worn over loose trousers.

On which there dances Ramadan's[1] new moon.
Perhaps this moon, on such a night as this,
Was witness as the Prophet scaled the peak
Of Hira[2] to recite the Holy Book.
Even tonight he might leave Paradise
And board that golden skiff, the moon, to sail
To earth and visit the assembly here.

Each new arrival's greeted by those there
According to the custom, *comme il faut*.
The mullah sits among them with his beard
So highly perfumed[3] that it seems he blows
Out clouds of incense and the breezes faint.
His face shines brighter than the Arab moon
As, Malud[4] in his hands, he reads how men
Of old conducted their affairs, a guide
For all believers now. First he describes
God's shepherd prophet: who can know what thoughts
Besieged his mind when sitting there alone
His head was whipped by wind, and desert dust
Rose up in clouds about him and his flocks
That gathered in acacia woods to graze.
A messenger came down from Paradise,
His body oiled with splendour, dressed in fire,
And in his hands he carried the Koran.
That day Mohammed stood on Hira's top
And 'Allah Akbar'[5] echoed round the world.

[1] *Ramadan* (the hot month), the ninth in the Moslem year, when strict fasting is enjoined during the hours of daylight. But eating may take place after dark. It is natural that a religious gathering (the nearest they get to a service after the Christian pattern) should take place in this month.

[2] It was in a cave on this mountain that Mohammed received his revelations. In fact the command Gabriel gave him when he received the first Sura was 'Recite', using a verb related to that used in the prophecy of Isaiah (40:6): 'A voice said, Cry. And he said, What shall I cry? All flesh is grass. . . .' Similarly the illiterate peasant Caedmon was ordered to recite (after the manner of the poets) before the Lord and thus produced the first religious poems in Old English.

[3] Perfume is much used by the men in Bengal; it is far from being considered effeminate.

[4] The *Malud* is the Moslem equivalent of the medieval *Golden Legend*, an account of the lives of saints and holy men full of moralizing advice.

[5] *Allah Akbar*, God is supreme.

Continuing his tale with tearful eyes
The mullah told of what degrading shame
The Prophet suffered at the scornful hands
Of infidels. He walked alone with God,
His picture in his heart, and in his hands
The Holy Book. Swords rushed above his head,
He braved the flashing blades of infidels
Surrounding him on every side like beasts.

> But his disciples said, 'As long as life
> Is ours we'll follow you wherever you may go.'
> The Prophet called, 'I'm not alone, my friends;
> I have an ally, none of you need fear.
> The smallest worm that hides beneath a stone
> Is known to God, and He provides its food;
> He is my hope, in Him I put my trust.'

Thus Manir Mitra followed him from birth
To death, describing each event that passed.
Hoisting religion's flag in holy war
The Prophet marched on Mecca once again,
Face bright as sun, hands shining like the moon;
With him disciples, heads held high, arms raised,
Ready to bow to none on earth but God.
The unbelievers cowered in their fear;
Farewell to earth if they came in his hands!

Someone bursts in just then. What news, what news?
Ask worried looks on faces old and young.
Up Madan Kulu leaps; what news, what news?
In wrestler's fashion folds his coat, prepared
For fight, and grasps his stick in knotted fists.
Running from somewhere Chadan Moral comes
With canes in bundles and a load of swords.
What news, what news? From nearby fields a cry
Arises howling like a Baishakh[1] storm,

---

[1] *Baishakh* (April 15th–May 15th), towards the end of which the monsoon
rains begin. The storms which often occur during this month are generally
accounted precursors of the monsoon proper.

Like rampant Meghna river's tidal waves,
Such waves as rush enraged and scatter foam,
Playing disaster's game on either bank.
The breast of night is robed with fire as torch
On torch is lighted; who is mad enough
To call the tune and dance disaster's jig?
These flames will burn the village and consume
Canal and river; fire will lick the sky
And still it will not weary or be quenched.

Rise up then, rise, all doughty fighting men,
Swords swinging at your waist, hands clasping canes;
Bring spears, fetch hatchets, beat the cymbals, dance
With shouts of 'Ali! Ali!' till from earth
To sky the air's confounded with the cry.
You must defend the village's good name;
This day of battle will become the test
Of skills at arms, the courage in your hearts.
Now they're approaching, those that seek you out;
Oppose their shouts with cries that answer back
Till 'Simul Toli' thunders from the clouds.
Let streams of fire descend the mountains, stir
The ocean to its depths of seething foam,
And bring disaster to your enemies.

    'Do us this favour, reverend sir; we clasp
      Your feet and beg you hold your words in check,
      Sealed in your mouth as in a closed Koran.
      Today we'll parley with the tips of canes
      And write out messages in our heart's-blood.
      We'll listen to your words on our return
      To Simul Toli and our former homes.'

'Only one word, one word you must obey
Before you gird your weapons on to fight.'

    'Obedience is not for us today,
      Nor is today the time for listening
      To you when deeds of valour must be done;

Shut up your book of words for later on.
It was on your advice we left our homes
And stole away like thieves without a blow.
Long generations of our ancestors
Dwelt there in Simul Toli and fought hard
To win and keep the glory of its name.
One word of yours made their descendants flee
From country bumpkins in a paltry band.
Now look at us; O sir, look what you've done:
The sons of tigers graze today like sheep
In others' fields; the frog hops fearlessly
On fangless serpents' hoods. Give them a chance
And these brave Namus marching on the homes
Of Kaji where we hide so shamefully
Would pinch the teeth out of our very mouths.
Whose rashness made them bold but those who fled
Them, creatures once so servile that lame flies
Could bite them without fear? Now it's our turn;
Tonight the boot is on the other foot.
The village name shall be redeemed, revenged,
Or else we'll die in the attempt and none
From Simul Toli shall be left to tell
Of the defeat before tomorrow's sun.'

'Nevertheless, one word you've got to hear.
Now I am old I look back on a life
Familiar with our village joys and griefs.
I lived in Simul Toli, eighty years
Acquainted with its sorrows, eighty years
Of counting its good fortune mine to share.
I was the one who called the gatherings
For prayer in every district and, concerned
As you for its good name, I was the one
Who read the Malud as your guide in life.
Once there was muscle rippling on my arm
When I was young and power swelled my chest;
Then it was fire that coursed along my veins.
If I were shaken now my ribs would crack,
But even so I'm not the one to skulk

At home, cowering in corners when there's work
To do. If you're resolved to fight then take
Me with you, and if I should die this way
Then there will be some honour in such death.'

'O honourable and reverend sir, inspired
By courage such as yours we'd like to lift
You shoulder-high and dance the village streets.
No one can conquer us now such as you
Have thrown aside your eighty years to join
The game of death. Who can oppose us now
When we advance and carry you with cries
Of "Ali! Ali!"? Reverend gentleman,
We'll fill our souls with Simul Toli's fame
And march undaunted when you give the word.'

'Take up your canes, this is no time for talk;
Jump to it, tremble land and tremble sky.
Look how the roaring Namus fill the field;
Sons of our village, dress in heroes' garb,
Rise like the storm and snake-like shake your hoods,
Rush into Kaji's fields and wield your canes.'

The men prepare with torches in their hands;
Beware! Beware! The storm comes fourteen ways
At once like Baishak's cloudy black monsoon.
Oil-presser Madan rushes in a rage
And dances in a circle round the group
Until collapsing in a grinning trance
He cries aloud the verses and the charms.

'Come Dak, come Dakini,[1] come rushing, run,
Devils and demons, ghosts and witches, come.
Where are you, black and stormy night of Hell?
Where are you, goddess with dishevelled hair,
Princess of darkness[2] in your wild attire?

---

[1] *Dak* and *dakini* are male and female imps, attendant upon Kali and nourished
by human flesh. Since a Moslem is speaking here, we have in his speech
another example of the Bengali cultural synthesis.

[2] Kali (the black one).

Prince Radhi,[1] prince of Hell, come rushing, come,
And leave your nether principalities.
With tawny matted hair come rushing, come
With the majestic pace of clouds, blind night;
Seal up the light at every compass point,
High hills and mountains, come, come rushing, run.
Gale at whose gust the coral tree is forced
To wave its crusted locks, come rushing, come;
South wind, the arbiter of speeding clouds,
Swoop swiftly down now, come, come rushing, run;
Kali of the cremation ground, swoop down
With sixteen hundred spirits in your train,
Come dancing swiftly, shaking like the grippe,
To join this tempest-tossed, this febrile game.
Come, Siva,[2] from the shivering north-east,
With incantations calling everyone;
And wrathful Chandi, Chandi with your child,
Avenging Durga,[3] come with shouting haste.'

Dust, dust, thrust up the dust in Ali's name,
Burden the mighty wind with flying motes
As we go rushing to the game of death.
Dust, flying dust, must cry exultantly,
The flying dust that smiles in private glee
And red as madness scatters streams of fire
Like glowing thunderbolts on every breast.
A mad *mélange*, loud sound, and storm and rain:
All Kaji village ringing with the cries
Of Mural Daho's 'Ali! Ali!'
Singing with 'Simul Toli! Simul Toli!'
Here come the raging Namus to be met
With 'Ali! Ali! Hazrat Ali!'
Brothers, come leaping, come, torches ablaze.

---

[1] *Radhi* sounds suspiciously like the Greek Rhadamanthus, the just judge of Hades. There is a pun here on the word *patal*, which means both 'prince' and 'underworld'.

[2] *Siva:* the name used is Ishan, which may also be used to refer to a stormy north-eastern wind, another pun.

[3] *Durga* is yet another name for Kali in her vengeful aspect.

The band of moslems rushes with a shout
Past Kalar[1] district through the Kaji fields.
Strike! Strike! They carry our their lives to pawn.
Strike! Strike! They issue out to meet their death.
They go out and Hell-fire is on their heads.
The night-wind trembles when it hears their din;
Their torches make the darkness seethe and writhe.

[1] *Kalar:* there is probably a species of wordplay here. The word can also mean doom and apply to a goblin in Siva's household. Compare the use of river names (first note in next chapter) and some of the place-names used by Isaiah (a master of word-play) and other Hebrew prophets.

CHAPTER 13

Mayna despises the vermilion of this place;
Save Dacca's none will satisfy her wilful need,
For wearing only that she thinks her body's cool.
    A formal turban in his right,
    His left hand holds a peacock fan;
Over the bride to be the bridegroom's body sways.

—Moslem girl's bridal song

Well I'm a king bee, baby,
    want you to be my queen,
Together we can make honey
    the world has never seen.

—Rhythm and Blues song

On the Gauri[1] river's banks a cottage stands;
An interwoven miracle of vines
Surrounds it with enchantment and cool shade.
Playing in sunlight, swaying in the wind,
Its blossoms flutter; wild flowers laugh convulsed
In every corner of the yard all day.
A trellising of beans, pumpkins and gourds
In clusters, wave their fruits in rivalry.
Beneath their stems the pot-herb *noté shak*[2]
Ripples in scarlet currents till it seems
Some lady's sari left out in the sun.
A waddling, clucking mother gullinule
Comes here at times, while in the forest trees

[1] *Gauri* (fair-complexioned) is a name for Kali in one of her better aspects; it suggests, therefore, the calmness and well-being of the following scene. Another significant use of a river name is the Kumar, over which Sojan and Duli swam to get to this haven. The name refers to Siva's younger son and may be translated prince, or even simply as child; but this prince is also a war-god. The flight, therefore, might be interpreted either as a leaving behind of childhood, or as an initiation into war since the attack on Kaji village follows immediately afterwards.

[2] *Noté-shak* is the red pot-herb growing in Maynamati's yard in Chapter 9.

The fearless birds are singing, unaware
Of any human habitation there.

Chilis and peppers, coriander seeds
Unhusked, peas, beans and lentils, spread with care,
Lie in the sun to dry. All colours, shades
And tints of chili, lentil, pea and bean,
Black pepper, coriander, brown, green, red,
Are mingled with designs in powdered rice
That weave and spell with love a secret story.
It seems as if dawn splendours tarry here
To marry with the evening's fleecy pink
A web of light that clouds transliterate.
A strutting peacock cottage spreads aloft
Two roof-wings and sits brooding over all;
It ducks beneath the darkling forest shade
And cunningly conceals its hiding-place.
The forest's god who left the plain in fear
Of men has stored creation's secrets here.
His slender consort, tired of sylvan play,
Has clasped the woodland's shadow round her form
And settled it according to her mind
As if she meant to sleep thus loosely dressed.

Below, legs stretched before her, sits a girl;
Black tresses frame the dado of her spine,
Fall floating to the floor. She brushes back
The strands a breeze has blown into her face
Relinquishing her hold upon the shelf[1]
Of coloured rope she's weaving with both hands;
But her impatient gesture breaks the thread.
With rolling angry eyes she scolds the twine

[1] This shelf is actually a shelf-substitute woven out of various materials
(hemp, jute, rope, netting) into which pots of various sizes, and other things as
well, may be inserted. It may then be hung across a room. It is better than a
conventional shelf since it gives added protection against insects, snakes,
rodents and other vermin. Since a village-girl is valued for her handiwork,
especially when it is a question of her becoming a bride, it serves as a useful
bit of self-advertisement. It will be noted later that Duli has one filled with
other handicrafts.

Then laughs at her stupidity at last,
Embroidering more finely than before.
Her leaf-dark face reflects the dusky vines
Whose love has smeared her body with their shade;
A woodland daughter, bound into its heart,
Enmeshing it with hers, herself a shadow,
Blends the bending shadows with herself.
Lost in such shade, lost in her thoughts, she weaves
Her tangled skeins beneath the cottage eaves.

Bound stretched across a Sundi bamboo[1] frame
Her skilful work progressed, a covering
With butterfly designs. The canework walls
Were tightly twined like snakes with here and there
Star-patterned glowing sparks. The floor was cooled
By mats spread out on reeds. The rafters gleamed
With clustered painted flowers, vermilion dabs,
A splash of turmeric; it almost seemed
The flowers were real. Tied at the ceiling was
A hanging shelf containing handicrafts.
One could not tell which were to be preferred,
The life-like flowers, the varied works of art.
There glittered china dishes, coloured phials,
Casting a rainbow as the bending breeze
Caught at the swaying hither-thither shelf.
Tied there an orchid creeper, star-shaped flowers,
A branch of flowering, shrub, excelling all.
Spreading a mat below, sitting slone,
The girl was weaving intricate designs.

This miscellaneous consortium,
The swaying shelf, the decorated beams,
The clustered vines, birdsong and forest tree,
All these create an excellence their own
Mingled together in the wilderness.
Uncomprehending still the girl goes on
Embroidering her butterflies and flowers,
Singing a song with low and gentle voice:

[1] *Sundi* bamboo is a fine variety used for art-work.

'Once upon a time in a distant land
The child-wife Bhanu in the depths of night,
Deep-lidded after endless games of dice,
Fell in the sandman's sack, the net of dreams,
Under the sway of the enchanter, sleep.

They lifted her into a palanquin,
They bore her off towards her husband's house;
Sleep-heavy, waking in her restless swing,
She looked in vain to find her family near.

Alas, where is that treasured mother now,
She who would sacrifice a buffalo
For no more than a thorn that pierced her foot?

Where would she find a father such as he
Who if her golden bangle merely bent
Would take it to the goldsmith's for repair?

Where was a sister so affectionate
That if her henna wore away she'd rub
Vermilion from her hair to guard her feet?

Was there another Maifal so beloved
To dandle in her lap; how would he fare,
That brother, in their playhouse all alone?'

Humming like this she sat while from far off
She heard the bride bird sing untiringly;
Closer it came, from the next paddy field,
Then from beneath the tamarind nearby.
Smiling with glee she put her work aside
And wooed it, 'speak, bride, speak, bo-katha-ko',
Then reapplied herself. Continually
It went on crying round the cottage walls
But still she bent, absorbed in weaving rope,
Foregtful of all else around but that.
From the direction of the door this time
It called, 'bo-katha-ko, bo-katha-ko,
Just turn your eyes this way and speak, bride, speak'.

The girl just smiled and went on weaving flowers.
The cinder-mouth now called right in her ear.

    'You rotter, ouch! Leggo, it hurts! All right,
    You win, I guess I heard that time; the bride
    Is speaking after all. Satisfied now?'
    'I thought bird-language was what all wives spoke
    And that life passed in calling branch to branch.
    But no, the poor old male can whistle till
    He bursts and get no chirrup in reply;
    The cinder-face just sits all day and weaves.'

'Get lost, you idiotic tub of words!
But what are you about? You've just got home
And now you take your axe and go again;
Why don't you rest a bit?' 'You get the rice
Prepared and I'll be back. I'm only off
To cut bamboo and bring a bundle home.'
'No, that won't do at all; just sit down first.'

    Quickly she rose to bring a sweetmeat tray
    Where curd and sesame and coconut
    Confections nestled in neat sugared squares
    Surrounded by a border of wild flowers.
    She filled with water a bell-metal cup
    So polished that it mirrored all the room,
    Then took a peacock feather and sat near.
    'Now you've a meal that's fit for gods to eat.'
    'But aren't you joining me?' 'I thought you'd know,
    To sit with Moslems would degrade my caste.'
    'Well, now I'm spoiling mine,' he said and eat
    With relish, simulating gravity.

Meanwhile his round-lipped wife was scattering sparks
Amid the swirling hubble-bubble smoke;
Ash flew about and settled on her face,
—Not though you'd notice any difference
For better or for worse. She puffed and blew,
Eyes popping and cheeks swelled, beneath his gaze,

Absorbed so much that he forgot to wash
His hands on finishing his meals. She saw,
However, as she laid aside the pipe
And turned on him, mock anger in her eyes.
At last she took her ropes into her hands
And recommenced her work. Neglectfully
Two henna-coloured feet pushed through her robe;
Two lotuses above the ocean's blue
Received the first of the dawn wind and bloomed.
Unwavering, without a blink or blush,
The boy sat staring till the girl perceived
And drew her feet away beneath her skirts.

Now Sojan fussed about and took his axe,
Making as if to go and fetch bamboo.
The elfin wife allowed her feet to show
Again as if she'd moved by accident.
He came and sat, pretending he had gone
To look for something that had slipped his mind.
Once more the feet were covered with the skirt
And he was left to puff his fuming pipe.

    'Look here, I'm sick of this; you weave all day.
    How long's this going to last? And by the way,
    This hookah isn't filled with water; pooh!
    It stinks high as a skunk, and it won't draw.'
    'But I just filled the thing.' 'Listen to me,
    You'd better mind you don't arouse the beast
    In me; if I get angry then you'll learn
    To watch your step. My head is throbbing, why
    Can't you close the kitchen door in all this heat?
    What's that you say? It's been closed all the time?
    Now look, you contradict my every word:
    It's bicker, bicker all the day. I'm sick
    Of it! I'm warning you, if I get mad
    You'll know about it soon enough, all right.'

'You grizzle over trifles all the time.
Now if you really mean to lose your temper

Why not let it rip? What's it to me
To see you roll your eyes when they grow red?'
'Oh, you're determined, then? Well that's all right
With me; you'll get your fun. No wife of mine
Shall say just what she pleases when she likes
While I'm around. Now look, this time I'll . . . no,
Ahem, well no, perhaps. . . . But the next time
You get my goat I'll show you what I'm made
Of and you won't escape so easily.'

> She laughed and put her weaving to one side,
> Well used to jocund scolding such as this;
> 'Sojan, my hero, how you've proved yourself!
> Now look at what I've painted on these walls:
> There Durga goes, the goddess Bhavani,[1]
> And this is Ganesh[2] with his single tusk;
> Now this is Radha sitting all alone
> Waiting for Krishna, though he's nowhere near.'
> 'Oh, why is that?' 'You are an idiot;
> Must I go over it again? He's gone
> Into the forest cutting wood.' 'Well then,
> Who is this funny fellow on the ox?'
> 'That's Siva, and you mustn't call him names
> Or he'll be angry if he hears of it.
> Now in this picture Krishna's on the path
> To Mathura,[3] and here King Ravana[4]
> Is driving in his demon chariot.

> This is Behula[5] floating on a raft

[1] *Bhavani* is Kali in her aspect as a mother-goddess.

[2] *Ganesh* is the elephant-headed but benign and very popular elder son of Siva. After the Jesuits had visited India wood-cuts of him began to appear in the black-letter compendiums on demons.

[3] *Mathura:* The scene depicted here may show Krishna quitting Radha in order to assume the kingly status for which he was incarnated.

[4] This demon has already been mentioned (p. 98). Here he may be represented as taking part in some episode from the famous epic, *Ramayana*, during which he kidnaps Rama's wife, Sita. The reference to Sita a little later definitely alludes to one of the most famous episodes in the *Ramayana* in which she follows her husband into his jungle banishment.

[5] The heroine of a favourite Bengali story in which this devoted wife journeys down the Gankini till means can be found to return her dead husband Laksmindar to life.

With dead Laksmindar's head upon her lap.
The wife's vermilion washes from her brow
Into the waters of the Gankini;
She wipes her eyes upon her sari's end.
Look now at Sita, burdened with her grief,
Banished the city by the king and queen,
Sitting with Ram, who keeps on looking back
Before they plunge into the wilderness.
What grief they undergo at every hythe;
The waters weep in sympathy, embrace
The banks both neck to neck with dashing waves.
Come now, your eyes are brimming; never mind.
Look over here, the famous temple site
Of Vishnu,[1] Lord of the whole universe,
At Puri; then a little to the right
You'll see there's Krishna's Vrinda[2] forest shrine.'

'There's nothing missing; you've drawn everything
Except the Moslem saints. Suppose they are
Annoyed at your neglect?' 'What's wrong with you,
Sand-blind or something? Look at what I've drawn
This side, and bow—it's Mecca's holy mosque.
Here is the battlefield of Karbala
Amid the flying sand while swaying skies
Collapse upon the river Farat's banks.
The tent of Hosein's here, and Sakina
Has heard about her husband's death and tears
Her wedding dress to shreds. Hosein himself
Is tearing at his breast and burns with thirst
But no one carries water at his call.
His relatives are mourning for his fall.
Sleeping beneath the mountain over here
Shiri and Farhad[3] lie; the forest trees

---

[1] Vishnu has, like Siva and so many other gods and goddesses, both a dark destroying aspect to his nature, and one that is loving and saviour-like. It is generally the latter that is most emphasized, especially through his avatars, Krishna and Rama. The famous temple at Puri in Orissa is dedicated to him and here the renowned chariot procession takes place.

[2] Vrinda forest (Vrindavana) is a Vaisnavite centre sanctified for its connection with the loves of Radha and Krishna.

[3] In historical fact Shiri (*Chirin*, the sweet) was an Armenian Christian,

Stand sentinel above their leaf-strewn tomb.
Beneath the shady pomegranate branch
Majnun and Laila grieve and share one grave.
Here's Simul Toli, here the village mosque . . .
But get along with you, dull heap of ash,
You keep me chatting and it's getting late;
Be good, annoint yourself and have a bath.'
The wife arose and slowly went to cook;
The boy arose and left the room to bathe.

> 'I'm off,' said Sojan, bundle on his back.
> 'Now don't forget to bring back what I asked.'
> A few yards on he turned and called his wife:
> 'Vermilion for the lady of the house?'
> 'Perhaps my lord and master's off his head;
> He brought it yesterday. Remember now?
> I wanted sunda, methi, turmeric,
> And catechu today; now don't forget.
> Over and over I asked you; I give up!¹'

He'd walked a little distance when she called:
'I beg my gracious husband turn around;

favourite concubine of Chosroes (Kushraw) II, King of Persia at the end of the sixth century. He eventually married her, and she remained a faithful wife right up to his assassination, after which she poisoned herself at his tomb. Legend has elaborated an earlier love of hers for one Farhad, an engineer responsible for driving a canal through the mountains to the King's summer palace. Despite the King's efforts to interfere with their romance they remained faithful until the King sent false news to Farhad that Shiri was dead, whereupon he threw himself from a mountain or, in some accounts, took poison. According to most legends the King then married Shiri himself and she remained faithful to death. Obviously Duli must be thinking of a still more concentrated version in which Shiri elects to kill herself at Farhad's tomb in the mountains. This is another example of Jasim Uddin's prophetic imagery.

¹ The shopping list consists of various spices and condiments, not all of which are in a ground form. Cinnamon comes as tightly rolled tubes of bark; cardamom as seeds; chilis as pods. In addition other leaves are used beside those of the bay. Surda and Methi are seeds ground for the sake of their oil. Catechu is a reddish paste sometimes spread on a betel leaf together with lime and slivers of the betal nut; the whole is rolled into a package an inch long and chewed like chewing gum. Duli addresses her husband formerly in the third person. A Bengali woman often speaks to him thus indirectly as 'my lord', and refers to him to the neighbours as the 'man of the house', much as Irish women used to speak of their husband as 'himself' and Victorian couples spoke of each other as Mr and Mrs.

Cardamom, chilis, sen-sen, cinnamon bark,
I'd like all these if you've enough to pay.
I meant to mention it, but I forgot.'
'I got all those only the other day;
Don't say you've scoffed the lot.' 'That's how it is,
He makes a note of everything I eat!
It's time his lordship learned two stones of spice
A day is what's required. Oh, one thing more;
I don't suppose you've heard, by any chance,
Of saris bordered with the bind-weed flower?
I know about the other ones, wave-wash,
Sand-bank, the rose-print and the timber-tree,
But I'm not interested in them; I have
A hankering to wear red Kolmi flowers.'

    'You've left the most important thing till last
    And told me in the very nick of time;
    You should have said before. I'll sell two stone
    Of jute and get it like a shot, you wait.
    Well, off to market now. Tie up the cow
    And bolt the cottage door when evening comes.'
    'Don't be late home. Stop turning round to look
    And get along or else you won't arrive.'

Thus do the waters of their happiness
Reflect their smiling days; the waves have washed
Away all signs of their unhappy past.
Sojan has taken up the woodman's trade
And every Saturday he goes to sell
His wares in Madjumalati marketplace.
And Duli practises her handicraft
At home, strings tiny beads for necklaces,
Weaving at whim, and sewing when she likes.
No other house is near; upstream and down
The boatmen idly float or fill the sails.
And now and then the helmsman leaves his helm
To drift like him upon the waves of song
That issue from some angle of the bank,
Flute-like, world-detached, and fancy-free.

CHAPTER 14

I wait and still he does not come;
I shut the world from my dark mind.
The fiery hells of parting glow;
There is no way to put them out.

In the hope of dark-skinned Krishna's coming
The couch is laid and the room is ready
And I have watched the whole night through.
Hopeless to hope, the people wake,
The Citizens of Braj[1] arise
And my dark mood shuts out the world.
—Song of Separation

I wait for the days to go by,
I long for the nights to go by,
I hear the knock on my door
          that never comes,
I hear the telephone
          that hasn't rung.
(Chorus) *You've gotta tell me you're comin' back to me.*
—Pop song

Sojan exclaimed one day, 'I cannot pass
My life forever in the woodman's trade.
I have become a partner in a boat
And mean to sail tomorrow to do trade
Some distance off. There's profit to be made
From selling jute; I mean to get my share.
Kedari's mother will stay nights with you.'

'We have each other; what's the use of gain?
I'd rather you stayed here and we were poor.
Besides, the Namus might discover you
Are living here and come to capture us.'

---

[1] *Braj* (Vraj) is the region associated with the love of Radha and Krishna.
This song, like so many of the folk songs dealing with separation, is put into the
mouth of Radha.

'No one will trace me and I'll be away
No more than six or seven days, you'll see;
I shall return, you have no need to fear.
There's heaps of money to be made in jute;
I'll bring you back a sari washed with waves,
A peacock feather, nose rings, necklaces,
And silver anklets to fit both your legs.
—That's why I'm sailing off, to fetch these things.
Your wrists are bare of ornaments, your nose
No richer for a jewel; you must not fear,
The distance is not far, I shall come back.'

He had his way and early the next day
The trader's vessel came for Sojan, raised
Its sail and disappeared into the haze.
Unhappy Duli hung up durba grass
And paddy on the fan for winnowing
And welcome; oil, vermilion, betel nut
She smeared upon the boat and then performed
The farewell ceremony. As she watched
The full-sailed boat set off and tacked downstream
To the far sandbank on the furthest lip
Of sky; into the blazing bur of mist
It went, the body mingling, then the sail,
Till all was lost behind a blur of tears.
Eye-bright with weeping Duli turned away,
Heart fluttering to the far horizon still.

Six weary days had plodded one by one
With not a sign of Sojan's coming home.
Idly the pitcher's filled, refilled again;
As many craft have tied up to the quay
And gone again; their waves have missed the shore
And splashed in Duli's heart. 'Where is he now?
What's happening? Why doesn't he return?'
They whisper as they wander, wounding her.

Kedari's mother sleeps nearby at night
But Duli keeps her room and stays awake

In case her husband should return home late.
She crushes henna for her feet and wears
A sapla flower behind her ear; she draws
A fine mascara line about her eye
And wipes the old vermilion from her brow,
Renewing it again; she rubs her palms
With violet seeds of pui[1] to redden them.
For who can tell when Sojan might return;
If he should see her in a dingy garb,
Dowdy plain Jane, she'd never bear the shame.
She folds her sari neatly, holds the glass
In front and watches that no wrinkle shows;
She chews chopped betel slivers till her lips
Glow red. When Sojan comes she will not speak
A word to him but sulk and skulk awhile,
Hide in a corner of the room and lower.
Thus occupied with small domestic thoughts
She lets the night pass by until the star
Of morning flies far off to hide her shame.

The burnished lamp that burns beside her bed
Reflects her body round and round its sides
And seems to mock at all her finery.
She pulls her chignon loose and throws away
The flower that graced her ear to watch it float
Upon the current of the ebbing tide.
Hopes spring eternal in her human breast
And scatter down a brightness on the boats,
For who can keep them bound? Like sandbank birds
They flutter free and take the empty paths
Of air with whirling cries and falling calls.

Today the past's enchantment captures her,
Parades its coloured ranks before her eyes;
All day she paints upon the cottage walls,
Rubbing vermilion, dabbing turmeric:
That night of darkness on the forest path,

---

[1] The *pui* is a creeper used as a pot-herb; it is usually children who rub the
seeds between their palms.

Pulling aside the creepers and the vines,
And ever at their back the scurrying
Of Namus in their hasty search with flares
That streamed before them through the jungle's rags
While she fled on with Sojan at her side.
That and another picture Duli drew,
Swimming the Kumar river on his back.

And then the farmer's house, his little child
Who looked up smiling like a crescent moon;
She never tires of Duli, shows her dolls
Or picks her flowers, and bringing her young calf
Insists she pet it. She is not afraid
To tell her where her hidden cowries are.
She cried and cried when Duli left and called
Her 'sister', said that if she ever came
That way again she must be sure to call:
     'And then I'll make you garlands of ripe gab,
     And when the basket-weaver comes I'll buy
     A tray of wicker-work; from gipsy wares
     I'll choose a coloured cradle for my dolls
     Which you will decorate with flowers and vines.
     In Baishakh when the mango branches bend
     Beneath the heavy fruit I shall expect
     A visit; I'll be cross if you don't come.'

Now Duli paints the burden on that tree,
And branches sagging through the netted leaves.
The farmer's daughter shades herself beneath
And strings a berry-garland of dark kuch;
Beside her lies a decorated tray.
And now she carefully delineates
That time she fell down fainting from the sun
And Sojan laid her on his lap and fanned
Her with a branch, leaned so she lay in shade.
Alas, they wandered like the river weed
That has nowhere to go; they never slept
In villages but shared the forest floor
With beasts. The watchman on the Ganda quay

Made eyes at her, flirted with flattery,
Till Sojan punished him and drove him off.
The tale of their escape fills all one wall.

Now Duli draws the Gauri with its sails
Of red and blue that bump and sway about
And journey to far lands. At the wharf edge
A lonely girl is waiting tearful-eyed
With pitcher on her hip. Here every line
Is heartfelt and embracing colours weep
Into each other, telling back the grief
That Duli feels within, as if a friend
Confiding sorrows similar to hers.

She was intent, she did not turn to see
People and police were standing at her door;
With them was Sojan, and his hands were bound.

CHAPTER 15

Bright buildings built of brittle brick
Rush on to ruin day by day.

>   —Baul song

Fierce bands of slaughter came together then,
The javelins rang aloud.
Loud sang the sombre, dewy-feathered bird
Among the spear-shafts, eager for the slain.

>   —Anglo-Saxon 'Genesis'

Now listeth[1] lords and ladies, least and most,
How Namus and how moslems fiercely fought
In battle bloody joined, and how they wrought
A plague on both their houses in the way.

One night of Magh in 1922
The Namus fell on Kaji, sword in hand;
One thousand shield-men swept down like a storm,
Their hatchets whirling in the torches' light.
Leaving the Malud meeting with a shout
All of the moslems rose and cracked the sky
With 'Ali! Ali! Ali!' Fires broke out:
You'd say the mark of Cain, the spot of hell,
Was glowing on the forehead of such flames;
Unnaturally bright and twice as hot
They seemed to girdle all the smoky earth.

Gathered together from the villages
Around came reinforcements at the run,

[1] Jasim Uddin uses the conventional ballad-singer's call to attention on the part of his audience. It also signifies a shifting from one element of the story to another and is, perhaps, a little less fussy than Chaucer's 'Now leave we Palamon and turn unto Arcite again, etc.'. The report of the fight that follows, however, in spite of its folklore elements, is supposed to be couched in terms of a military communiqué.

The print of fire enflamed upon their hearts.
Nayeb the sympathetic seemed inclined
To favour the attackers for he sent
The men of Telihati to their aid.
Madhabodiya rose, and Keshtapur;
Mohanpur's menfolk hurried like a swarm
Of locusts to support the Namu side.

When the Nawab of Dacca heard of this
He sent a thousand moslems in reply
To even out the overwhelming odds.
They crossed the river Padma, and the sky
Was blackened by the host, the light was dim
Until they passed. Kazem the killer came,
The same who takes a bullet in his mouth
And shouts on Ali's name and is not harmed.
Chandan the wrestler came, his skin so tough
Even a fishing spear can't penetrate;
He'll fight a week and never seem to sweat.
And Bachan Mitra came; when he recites
The Holy Book a thousand men with canes
Fall prostrate at a puff and do not rise.

Gadai the fighter led the Namu side;
None can compare with him: He'll hurl a spear
Across eight fields; an arrow from his bow
Is like forked lightning rushing through the sky.
Ram-hati came; he's only got to beat
His chest to cause an earthquake; thunder roars
About the mountains like a Baishakh storm.
Heroic Nidhi Ram, true to his name,
His skin as tough as boar's hide; he can chew
The bullets in his mouth and swallow them
As if they were puffed wheat;[1] he puts an end
To every fighter in his knife-blade's range.
And Mahan Ray, flown by the eastern wind,

[1] Bengal is a rice-eating district; they have even refused shipments of wheat
during famine. The equivalent of popcorn is a puffed rice, a sort of 'rice-
crispy'.

Swooped down to scatter charms; he brought a train
Of sixteen hundred devils red as fire,
And demons dancing round him as he flew.

Days passed with heavy fighting[1] on both sides;
Day after day Namu and moslem grew
More drunk on war. They burnt down villages,
Left not a house, ravaged the coutryside.
It doesn't seem to make much difference who
Is moslem, who is Namu now; all kill
Without discrimination. 'There he goes,
Catch, kill, kill brothers, catch him, here he is!'
Like maddened insect suicides some men
Set fire their clothes and immolate themselves.
The nursing babes are snatched from mothers' breasts,
Their brains dashed out with stones; women with child
Are ripped up with a scythe—atrocities
Committed in the name of war to spread
The fighter's fame on every path and hythe.

A cry of woe rose up and filled the land;
It will not cease until the Judgement Day.
Day and night, pyre on pyre, pyre after pyre;
How many mothers, pale with sorrow, weep
Preparing them? You'll find, look where you will,
Not men, graves only. Jackals pad around,
And cruising through the sky, vultures and kites.
The days rolled by, flames on the pyres grew low,
New sprouts of durba grass pushed through the graves,
But no green thing would comfort the tombed hearts
Of those unlucky ones whom war had left
To live with lonely sorrow all their lives.
Wind scattered only ashes from old pyres.
But in the heart the fires that will not die
Were fanned by memory's breeze to twice their heat.

[1] Jasim Uddin has had direct experience of religious rioting of this kind. He
was once almost killed but, at the last moment, a farmer cried out, 'Don't
kill him, he's our poet'. Thus does a desire for immortality soften the soldier,
and it is even as Robert Graves says: 'The indirect proceeds from poem-
writing can be enormously higher than the direct ones!'

Nayeb so sympathetic, what of him?
His sorrow for the people was so great
He dispossessed the victims of their homes
And ordered that a market should be built
Where what remained of Simul Toli stood.

CHAPTER 16

What wondrous workings in man's engine house;
Turbines of blue pass news from nerve and vein.
Upon the housetop burns a jewelled lamp,
Through all the inner rooms there shines great light.

—Baul song[1]

*The world is a wonderful place
    to be born into
if you don't mind some people dying
    all the time
or maybe only starving
    some of the time
which isn't half so bad
    if it isn't you.*

—'Pictures from the Gone World', Lawrence Ferlighetti

What news, what news? What news in passing, spoken news,
    News flying in the wind; its sound is fine.
News whispered ear to ear, winked eye and lifted brow;
    News rushes, troubling minds and breaking hearts.
News lags behind, news goes before, news here, news there,
    Some come to hear and others carry it.
Some news is true, a lot is false, they hurry it
    From market to the house; sometimes it brings
A touch of joy, sometimes it wails a song of grief.
    News passes through the outer court, news trots
Inside and prints a line of letters with belled foot.
    A one-horse carriage travelling down the road,
News comes, news goes; all are so occupied with news
    They haven't time to notice what it is.

[1] A *Baul* song is characterized by a slightly eccentric religious enthusiasm. It is sung by an itinerant minstrel, known as a Baul, treated with great reverence for his having given up worldly possessions and taken up the ascetic life.

We've heard that rent-collector Nayeb filed a suit,
        Had Sojan jailed on a wife-stealing charge.
They say that he was tried and given seven years;
        It may be true, who knows? When he was freed
He heard from everyone how Duli's happy now,
        Married to someone new. He could not face
Returning to his people with this grief and left
        The district, travelling in some gipsy boat.
Of course, you can't trust everything you're told, though it
        May hold some grain of truth; be it as may,
That's history; and anyway, who's interested?

News, news, forever new, it's borne along the path
        Like leaves before the wind; some wizard pulls
A net and we no longer see today what seemed
        There yesterday. The landlord's market fills
The site of Simul Toli like a monument
        Commemorating Nayeb's business skill.
Where have the Namus and the moslems gone today?
        Kazem the killer's voice is heard no more
Shrilling to battle; Madan's sold his axe to pay
        The landlord's taxes, and the edge has left
The fishing spear of Nidai Pal, old Sadhu's son.

Who fears the fame of Namu and of moslem now?
        Obsequious, they bow at Nayeb's feet;
They grovel in the dust to pass the time of day,
        Forgetful of the honour of their name.

CHAPTER 17

I roar like lions for their food.
I swagger and I beat about
As drunken mercenaries do.

The mountain must bear my whole weight.
For sharpening my blade I use
The shoulder of an elephant.

—Gaming Verse

If you see me coming better step aside;
A lot of men didn't and a lot of men died:
One fist of iron, the other of steel,
If the right don't get you then the left one will.

—'Poor man's blues'

Through Kaji's centre flows a small canal,
A glass in which the village sees itself.
The road from Simul Toli market runs
Along one side across the harvest fields
Like a broad scarf. The other side a path
Humps up and down, wounded where cattle pass,
Heaving and sighing in the dust they raise.
Along the market path an old man walks
Alone, a thousand sorrows deeply carved
Into his brow; he walks a little, sits
Again to rest, no longer strong enough
To drive his weary body on its way.

His mirror image on the other bank
Totters with eighty years of grief like his.
'Who is it walks that side?' he calls across,
'Gadai of Simul Toli,' the reply;
'Who speaks to me?' 'Chamir the warrior.
Do you remember how it used to be

When we were brothers in the village once?'
'Chamir, I'm glad. We haven't long to live,
But I've a wish to swap a tale or two
Although death's vulture hovers at my head.
It would be good to talk to you again,
Dear friend, before the end. Perhaps we have
All cursed and wished each other in the grave
Times without end. But I have suffered much;
I've laid my seven sons on funeral pyres
And yet it seems my sins pursue me still.'

'Don't bring that up again. What's done is done.
You're only rubbing salt into old wounds;
Why shut the gate after the horse has gone,
What use is crying over milk that's spilt?'

'No, friend, I want revenge, I want it now,
On him who dressed us up in poor men's rags.
I was the fool who followed his command
And gathered seven hundred of our men,
And what's become of them? In every lane
Of golden Simul Toli you will find
The landlord's market stalls.' 'But what revenge
Is open to you, Gadai? No one's left;
Our brothers' graves cover the countryside.
The mullah's house, that symphony of roofs,
Houses the vendors now; there they hold court,
Bustling about in his reception room.
Great baskets fill the space of seven rooms
Where there were folk whose harvests overflowed
The courtyard. But there is no family left
To light the lamp at evening; all of them
Lie sleeping in the earth of Kaji now.
On whom, then, will you take revenge today?
Chamir the warrior no longer takes
The cane up in the cause of anyone.
My arms, no longer strong, hang at my sides
And I've no better thing to do than sit
Beside the graves and reckon up how long

Before the coming of the Judgement Day.
But what revenge have you in mind, old man?
There was a time each quarter built its huts
Under the friendly shade. We used to dance
To Gajan songs[1] beneath the kindly trees.
Did we not drag the plough from field to field
As far as the Rai pond? Those were the days,
Such days as made work seem like festival.
Namu and moslem, where are they today?
The streets are empty, no one lives there now.
They passed as surely as those days through pyres
Whose flames were spent, whose ashes scattered long
Ago; and deep beneath the wormy earth
They dwell in darkness. Call a thousand times,
Cry till your throat is hoarse, no answer comes,
And none will stir for all your sighing breath.'

'I want revenge, I'll have revenge on him;
I've kept this worn-out body from the brink
Of death to mete out punishment on him.
His were the orders brought us down so low
And yet in all our conflicts felt no blow,
Whose body went uninjured by so much
As one poor straw in all our cut and thrust.'

'If such is fate's decree who can avoid
What's written, friend? I know the world's wry ways.'
'No, brother, I will take revenge for that.
My life's been spent in wandering grief's land
Because of what "*they*" did. If "*they*" remain
Alive they'll use the opportunity
To set the Namu on the moslem once
Again in the near future. One of these,
At least, who profit from our quarrelling,
I'll drag with me between the hands of death.
I should be proud to die in such a cause.
Only give me the chance to lay my hand
On Nayeb, that satanic hypocrite,

[1] *Gajan* songs are sung at the *Chorok* ceremony mentioned in Chapter 2.

And send him gibbering into death's vale
And I'll assume my grave-robes with a smile.'

'What's that you say! I do not understand.
Ram Nagar's rent-collector; isn't he
The Namus' friend?' 'The Namus' friend, that's what
You think! The favour that he shows consists
Of letting us kneel down to take the dust
Before his feet. We are inferior
To cats and dogs to him, beneath contempt.
Our backs are bent, our bones are sore, our life
Is spent under the shadow of his rod.
He reared himself a palace of our ribs
And drew his lordship's carriage on our heads.
He whom we're forced to honour was no friend
To any man, whatever was his creed.
If any be the Namus' friends they are
The ones who plough the fields, bathing in sweat,
Baked by the heat of the Chaitra sun;
It's those whose cottages lie side
By side with ours, who share our lives come rain,
Come storm or shine, in sorrow or in joy.
They are the thousand farmers who are drawn
To life-long troubles as the moth to flame,
Upon whose heads the rains of Sraban[1] fall
Without respect for persons, equally,
As equally the landlord's punishments.
When you are poor it makes no difference,
It doesn't matter who or what you are.
For all our fighting, what was the result?
We sowed: death was the fruit we harvested;
The pyre claimed some, and some sleep in the grave.
From your eyes sorrow flows, and grief from mine,
Both streams are bitter and they taste the same.
But "*they*" have got their market and are glad.
Revenge, I want revenge; if I don't have
Revenge my mourning heart will never cease
To wail, not even after I am dead.'

[1] *Sraban*, July 15th–August 15th.

144

Then Chamir girt his loins and took fresh heart.
'Namu and moslem are now reconciled.
We see each other in a better light;
New understanding breaks on both our minds.
The countryside is scattered with old graves
But still our brothers live within our hearts,
And though the pyres have died their flame still burns
There. Let us clutch it nearer, let us smear
That burning liniment upon our limbs;
Comrades in arms, we'll take whatever comes
With new-found strength that scorches through our
          veins.'
'My seven sons have passed on through the flames
And of the thousand villagers I knew
Not one now answers and I call in vain.
Their blood cries out, and they shall be revenged.'

Two men are walking, one on either bank.
Pictures of day are trampled underfoot;
The killer sun of evening stalks away.
Early next morning farmers walked that way,
Surprised to notice on one bank a grave
Fresh dug, and on the opposite a pyre.

News! News! What news? A village rumour has
It that no trace of Nayeb can be found.
After some time men digging by the pond
Found half his body buried in its bank;
Crowds came to wonder, gaping and amazed.

CHAPTER 18

I did not know before, love steals the soul;
If only I had known it was like this.
I'll write this letter to my friend and say
    I did not know before.

The one who loves must burn in rice-chaff smokes,
In desiccated cow-dung's scorching fire,
Though ignorant before, ignoring afterwards.
    I did not know before.

How long shall I remain bound inextricably
Between the warp and woof of love's straw frame,
Behind the bolted door of love's thatched house?
    I did not know before.

I cut my finger; it becomes a pen;
My bitter tears are good enough for ink;
For postman's satchel, here's my broken heart.
    I did not know before.

        —Murshida Song

Now that you are not with me
    I know what love is.
    Now—you know?—now
That you have shut the door
And the shadow of my hand
Remains caressing your absence.

—*Pequeños Canciones*, Fernando Garcia Bravo

Along the Madhumati river sails the fleet
    Of gipsies, dashing waves against the shore.
Sons of the soil who sulked and left their mother's lap
    Taking to nameless rivers and the swing
Of waves. On either side the land runs after them
    With shores outstretched like arms, but till this day,
Alas, her restless children have evaded her.

She calls them back along the wooded paths,
      She woos them ceaselessly with cool green shade, the fields
Of paddy like a rice-paste painting, fruit
And flower-filled villages. But not for dancing ponds
      Of light, the red dust flying down the roads,
The Gajan market—anyone's enchantment, will
      They turn their face for an abode on earth.

Their floating village perches on the tide and sails
      From river into river with no end
To journeying, no boundary to stay its course.
      Love and affection's magic float with them,
Fondling caresses eddy round and shadow them;
      The waterways are loud with fighting talk,
Renunciation's greatness, virtue's victory.

Who has raised up a novel world on water here
      And pulled it to and fro for eye's delight?
The foremost boat unbalances, the helm swings round;
      The wife stands up against the coloured sail
That bellies in the wind. Below the thatching sits
      Her husband carving flowers upon a stick,
Hair blown acrosss his face. In that boat over there
      The husband hurls his wife onto the boards
And beats her; next to them a couple play at cards
      And take no notice. Kurukshetra's[1] field
Is re-enacted on another where the fight
      Of wife and nagging mother's never done;
And further on a husband leans to his love's ear,

[1] *Kuru-kshetra* is the culminating battle between the Pandavas and Kuravas
(symbolizing the forces of light and darkness) as told in the other great Indian
epic, the *Mahabharata*. It is at this point of the story that the more famous
interpolation, the *Bhagavad Gita* (blessed song) is introduced. A good deal of
punning is going on here. Juan Mascaro, in his translation of the Gita, intro-
duces the Sanskrit meaning of the battlefield's name as 'The field of Truth,
the battlefield of life', but the word can also be used in connection with a
domestic squabble, as here. Needless to say, no Hindu would dream of making
such a low image out of a literary and religious classic. I suppose, however,
one could count this as an instance of the mock-epic image and compare it with
The Battle of the Frogs and Mice (ascribed to Homer), that eclogue of Virgil in
which Augustus' court is compared with the economy of a bee-hive, Dryden's
MacFlecknoe and Pope's *Dunciad* and *The Rape of the Lock* (and Joyce's *Ulysses*).

He playful, whispering, and she entranced.
Dove's coo and call of gullinule, the kora's cry
      That threatens rain, the noises mix and clash:
The racket of a market ringing down the stream.

In several boats torn quilts are drying in the sun,
      In others bannered saris flap about;
Smells of dried fish waft here, and over there
      Sunda and methi seeds are ground for oil.
The evening lamps are lit at no fixed place; they wave
      By wharf and hythe their golden tinsel trail.
The village has no name, its territory spreads
      As far as rivers flow, as wide as sky;
Their neighbour is the sun, and in their love the moon,
      The stars and planets gather in a band
To journey with them. River shark and crocodile,
      Attendant fish in hosts, moor for the night
About the dinghy sides to share their company.

Down Madhumati river floats the gipsy fleet.
      All kinds of toys, glass bracelets, oyster pearls,
Chinese vermilion, peacock feathers, coloured beads,[1]
      Load down their boats and fill their tray of wares.
From boat to boat tame birds are whistling, chickens cluck,
      Cocks crow, where goats and hunting dogs are tied.
A baby cries upon its mother's lap while there
      Beneath the thatch the merry children play.

On sails the gipsy convoy. Children stand on shore
      And stare with wonder at this water-borne
New world, some waving, others singing nursery rhymes,
      And as they dance and play both shores resound.
The convoy passes Kajal-Kuthi's boundary
      And reaches Ujani; now they have sailed
By Goda-gari, past Bau-Ghata, quay of brides.

[1] The gipsy merchandise is of better quality than it sounds at first. The pearls
are probably the famous Dacca pink pearls; Chinese vermilion is the best of all
in quality; and the beads are made from Kashmiri semi-precious stones, such as
agate and lapis-lazuli.

They're leaving Loha-juri on their right
And come to Dharma-hata, mooring for the night
      By Uran khali's sandbank as the moon
Climbs overhead and ushers misty evening in.

Slowly then, very slowly in each boat the lamps
      Go out, soft noises are diminished, rocked
To sleep; the night breeze rushes here and there to catch
      The whispering of maiden and young man.
Now even susurrating sibilance is quenched,
      All squeak and titter soothed; the lunar jar
Pours down its radiance on earth like glossy dew.
      Cloud fibres trace their threads on heaven's screen
And brush by moonbeams. Crying now and then from far
      The cuckoo-hawk[1] is searching for his mate
And builds a path of melody between the earth
      Into the endless distances of sky.

The curtain of this silence parts. Now is the time
      The scorned neglected past plays at revenge,
Dealing a lonely hand of thumb-blacked old regrets.
      Someone is playing on a flute of reed:
The rolling notes are scattered on the sand; some fall
      Into the river, some take to the air
And in a chariot of moonray sleep on cloud.
      Such is the tune it seems to clutch a grief
The world itself could hardly bear. Again it wails
      As if it reached up hands to touch God's throne.

            Is there no end to wandering,
            Prisoner to eddying and ebb,
                  All for your cruel sake?
            Must I forever float downstream
            As in a Bhatiali song
                  The rootless water-weed?
            I bear my tray from part to part

---

[1] The cuckoo (or *kokila*) is the bird of love, since it sings in the spring. It was
similarly thought of as a popular bird in very early English and Arabian poetry
before it was ousted by the nightingale (or *bulbul*).

And still you have not sent me word
        Nor let me see you once.

Into the wood the wild bird flies,
That winger of great distances;
        I ask him if he knows
What place it is where Duli hides,
The object of this fruitless hunt;
        If he will bear her word
Even today the searcher lives
And still he sails from stream to stream,
        Pain's burden on his heart.

Bird swinging in the highest branch,
Turn your long-sighted eyes that way
        And tell me what you see.
Then fly to her, sparrow, fly,
And bring me where my dear love is
        While there is time to find.
My reed-frail coracle of life
Cracks, springing leaks; my earthen lamp
        Is flickering and dies.

Time struggles on; I must attain
To see her once again and then
        Let no one after ask
'What was this Sojan, who was he,
Where did he live, where has he gone?'
        This once, what shall I care
Then if they hear no news of me?
They say my heart's rose decks the wreath
        About another's neck.
The pity of it, little bird!
If that be so, how can hope live,
        How can I hope to live?

River, your current rushes past
Bucking to tunes the down-tide plays;
        Perhaps you know the place.

Then bear me now and take me there
Where I shall touch upon the shore
    On which I'll breathe my last.
And when I hear the throbbing song
The water in her pitcher makes
    Swaying upon her hip
I'll gladly close my tired eyes
And draw the sweet air deep to sing
    My funeral song and die.

The lesson that you teach is cruel,
Your twelve-month kisses crumble down
    The lips of both your banks;
While weaker subjects wear away
And leave you triumphing alone
    Your rough endearments thrive.
But had I learnt the truth before,
That love is so much suffering,
    Never would I have strayed
Beneath the flowering kadamba
Or plucked its branches for a wreath,
    This noose about my neck.

The dry dung burns with searing heat,
My body wilts; why does my soul
    Cling obstinately still?
A blow on water wounds the shore;
But I sustain that hurt alone
    There is no friend can share.
From door to door flickers the news
Of forest fire[1]; but who can know

---

[1] Forest fire and a river bursting its banks are frequently paired images with a literary history stretching back into Sanskrit verse when, very often, they stood as images of cruelty. The forest fire image at the end of Chapter 5 might also stand for this. In the lines here we might have an example of Jasim Uddin's borrowings from popular songs, a technique to which he admits although he is not very forthcoming about particular sources. The images appear to take their origin from a song often attributed to Chandidas. Here, for instance, is the

What flames of double heat
Are withering my heart away?
Trembling alone, I live, alas,
There is no remedy.

The windy sky received the words and understood
    Such weeping tones as, heard, would wound again
The bitter heart that uttered them and draw fresh tears.
    For miles the sandbank stretched on either hand,
Encoffined by the moon's pale planks. The final breeze
    Before the quaking dawn began to stir
And whisper its last messages on dusty breath.

second stanza of Deben Bhattacharya's version (lyric no. 6 in *Love Songs of Chandidas*, Allen & Unwin, 1967):

Water may kill a small fire
But how can I fight the holocaust
Of heart?
A burning forest rouses the world
Through flames,
But the embers of my heart
Ignite unseen.

The whole of Sojan's song could well be a patch-work of such borrowings.

CHAPTER 19

Fire at my heart, you will not die,
You flicker and you flicker on;
What oceans can extinguish you?
Fire at my heart you will not die.
The hunted deer[1] is free from guilt
Though her flesh has made the world her foe.
Fire at my heart, you will not die.

—Murshida song

Valve cannot vent the strain
Nor iron ribs refrain
The furnace in the heart.

—C. Day Lewis

Weed wanders with the river down the stream;
    Let no one ask of Duli now,
Let her forget what bitter paths she's walked.
    Are there not plenty who have borne
A thousand sorrows and a thousand pains?
    Their number burdens down the earth,
But who is eager to hear news of them?
    Are there not nameless birds and flowers
Whose lives are filled with little joys and cares?
    Let him investigate who has
An inclination for the filigree
    And leisure for such random facts.
Stars fall sometimes from skies that overflow;
    Should one such drop before your feet
You'd be hard-put to say from whence it came.
    Life's river curves this way and that,
It sees a thousand changes on its banks:

---

[1] The deer is, from Sanskrit times, the symbol of a person beset about with troubles.

Do not remind her of the past
And open up old wounds upon her heart.

She has endured a hundred times more pain
        Than human clay was meant to stand.
Fire in her heart is robed away from sight,
        A black snake[1] is her ornament.
She has passed through such summer's heat as burned
        The bride's vermilion from her brow.
Now she is tired; let her forget all this.
        Come sleep, the knotted hair is loosed,
Compartment misty night with golden dreams;
        Come sleep, lightner of weariness,
Enchant the microcosm and shut out
        The footsteps of the heavy world
That takes from this unhappy village girl
        The peaceful flowering of her life.
Let laughter come for ever fresh, and song
        Trip constantly upon her lips,
Steering the ferry boat of night and day.
        Evening and morning, let them come,
Twin sisters bathing in a pastel stream
        As if they'd charm her to forget,
As if this hapless girl could hide her past,
        Bruised, torn and gored, never at ease,
Along the path by which they come and go.
        Yet she proceeds unwillingly,
For ever looking back along the way
        Down which old griefs are vanishing.

Past sadness leaves its flavour in the mouth
        As if its touch had somehow changed
The quality of things, brushing the cheek
        With softer smiles, and echoing
Upon the ear in unfamiliar songs.

[1] The black snake is, one supposed, a cobra. Why Duli should wear such an ornament is open to various interpretations. A sign, perhaps, that she is now acting like an orthodox Hindu. Or, in view of the context, an emblem of her psychological state. She bears inside her a burning poison hidden from sight although, unlike the cobra, she does not mean to inflict it on others.

Now Duli will forget all that,
Her home encircled by the forest shade,
    Father and mother that she loved,
Names never to be mentioned any more.
        She will forget her childish games,
She will forget along which river bank
    They built their nest and like two doves
Enfolded one another with their wings.
        She will forget the district police
And what she had to testify in court
    Before the judge, the cruel strain
Of which had made her faint. Sojan was sent
        To jail on that auspicious day.

Her hands and feet were bound with ornaments,
    They beat the marriage drums again.
It is as if the story were not hers,
    As if some female mendicant
Had sung this song along the village path
    Playing upon the sarinda;[1]
Now she has gone the memory remains,
    Now even that she will forget,
And as for Sojan—God! the bogey man![2]
    May lightning break upon his head
Falling from every angle of tall skies.

'What sin did you commit to cause this pain,
    Friend in the trials that we shared?
The tears you shed are mingled with my own.
    If I had known before, my love,

[1] The *sarinda* is a short fiddle played by the lower classes, generally having a wooden body. The most likely version of this is the rudimentary North Indian sarangi, which is hollowed out of a single block of wood with a waisted front covered with skin, and a short, broad, unfretted neck into which tuning pegs are inserted laterally. This has three or four bowed strings (of gut) and from eleven to fifteen wire strings which resound sympathetically (as in the sitar and several other instruments).

[2] The bogey man (*Bhogoban* here) crops up wherever there are remnants of Indo-European myth, cf. the Nordic troll Boyg, and the Scottish boggle or goblin. Buonaparte, under the anglicized name of Old Boney, was used as a threat to children because of the similarity in name.

Love's fruit would turn to ashes in the mouth
    And that its tree bears thorny flowers[1]
I would have pulled it up with my own hands
    And laid the axe to root and branch.
Why was I born? Why did my mother not
    Put salt into my mouth at birth?[2]
For then she would have spared the innocent
    The consequences of my acts
Which bring with them misfortune, guilt, and pain.
    Was this your doing, angry gods,
To give this harmless girl such evil chance?
    Was I too happy that you drown
Me thus repeatedly in sorrow's sea?
    What offspring of the mother bird
Did Duli take, leaving an empty nest?
    What evil have I done that draws
A curse[3] down to pursue me all my life?
    Whose heart have I afflicted thus
To feel its smart inflicted on my own?
    Ravanna's everlasting pyre
Burns day and night there for no cause I know.

'Alas, whom did I injure with my love?
    Did my sighs sink some merchant's boat;
Who claimed my tears had overflowed his ground?
    How was I guilty, cruel gods?
Was it my frosty fears that nipped the buds,
    My burning fevers parched the crops?
Is this the reason that you brand my brow?
    If I could see you I would ask
If you have ever suffered pain like mine.
    O ruthless hunters that you are,
What poisoned arrow did you use to kill
    The wild deer with; do you perceive

---

[1] Compare with this the Western rose imagery.

[2] A neat way of choking an infant since the salt would eventually dissolve leaving no tell-tale traces.

[3] The Hindu Duli is here wrestling with the problem of karma or conditional destiny, the doctrine that suffering is caused by evil deeds in this life or (though this does not occur to her) in a former life.

The agony in which you let it die?
        Yours were the castes that keep the world
Apart, yours were the social barriers,
        The instituted hates that cause
Disruption, wars and riots, maiming, death.
        Widows and orphans turn on you,
All you bereaved, with curses on their lips.
        Why don't you recognize the need
Of longing souls that call to other souls;
        Why don't you sympathize with them?
Castes of the heart matter far more than mere
        False pride and accidents of birth.'

Duli will never utter all these thoughts
        Again; let her forget for good.
The new vermilion glows upon her brow,
        Conch bangles clash upon her wrists.
Her husband's name shines brighter than the moon.
        The sky could not contain her love
For him when he stands tossing back his hair;
        Even the gods would envy him.
Her granary is full of rice, crops crowd
        Into her courtyard all twelve months.
Rite follows close on festival; one goes,
        Another comes to take its place,
And in their midst she fashions images
        Of clay for all with skiful hands.
She distributes herself in restless toil;
        This is her life: this way she fills
The gap with healing, expiates the past.

CHAPTER 20

Have you more sorrow still,
More grief to give, O cruel one?
As a dumb man fares who sees a dream
And keeps it to himself,
Such is my fate, such is my lot,

—Murshida song

With serving still   *This have I won,*
For my good will   *To be undone;*

And for redress   *Of all my pain*
Disdainfulness   *I have again.*

And for reward   *Of all my smart*
Lo, thus unheard   *I must depart.*

—Sir Thomas Wyatt

Before the morning came the band
Of gipsies overflowed the streets
And bartered as they walked along,
Chinese vermilion, coloured toys,
Bangles of glass. The little boys
Ran out, as many girls flocked round,
Vied with each other calling them
And keeping pace, in front, behind,
A jolly jostling swarm of bees.
One pulls them here, one pulls them there,
Visit this house, or visit that.
One buys an ankle ornament
And shows it everyone with pride.

A little girl is overjoyed
To own a nose-ring made of brass.
Pulling and clinging at her skirts

Her baby brother frets and whines,
    'You bought a bangle, but my wrists
      Have nothing on; it isn't fair.
      I will not have it, that I won't.'
    'Who heard of bracelets for a boy?
      Better than that, you come with me
      And we'll pick pomegranate flowers.
      We'll gather unripe gab and string
      The seeds when we get home. I'll make
      A necklace for you, if you like.'
The naughty boy would not be still
Until they'd bought some trifling thing,
A whistle made from beaten tin,
Exchanging with the gipsy girl
Six pounds of rice, to satisfy
His honour for the sake of peace.

The second wife is cross today;
Mother-in-law had bought a gift
Of bangles for the little girl.
The mischief-making elder wife
Put chili seed and capsicum[1]
Into the dhal instead of salt.
The third wife broke her conch-shell brooch
As she was winnowing the rice.
Old grandmother, the household head,
Is tired of trying to keep the peace
And bargaining the price of goods.

Quarter to quarter gipsies go
Awaking harmony or strife,
All trooping down the paths with noise
That turns the village upside-down.
Burble, burble,[2] yap, yap, yap,
They speak what no one understands;

---

[1] Chili and capsicum seed are very hot; they have their place in curry making, but not in large quantities. Dhal are lentils.

[2] 'Ili, mili, kili', nonsense words, in the text. It is like the 'bar-bar' noise made by foreigners whom the proud and contemptuous Greeks dubbed barbarians.

Their riotously coloured robes
Stream after them upon the wind.
Village on village, as it seems,
Is caught in their enchanter's net.
This, that, and the other house
They visit carelessly and leave,
Strewing disorder on their way.
Their arms are many-bangled, brows
Anointed with vermilion, necks
Stringed round with beads; down from their lobes
There dangle ear-rings, in their nose
They're wearing nose-rings, round their legs
The anklets bell. In every house
They wake a wild festivity.
With many-tinted rivalry
And swinging step the gipsy youths
And maids invade the village ways.

> 'Who is it coming at this hour,
>   Bathed in sweat from the hot noon sun?
>   Sister-in-law, you call him here
>   And tell him he can come and rest
>   Beneath the shady Kadam tree.'[1]
> 'The Kadam's boughs are bent down to the path
>   Under the heavy blossom's weight.'
> 'Then call him over, bring him here,
>   Tell him he can sit in the living room.'
> 'On that large earthen floor the rats
>   Have pushed the soil up here and there.'
> 'Then tell him he can spread his mat's
>   Cool grass this side the courtyard wall.
>   —Gipsy, you're new; I've not seen you before.
>   Open your basket, let me see
>   If you have anything worth-while.
>   Now what about some yarn, or fine

---

[1] Duli's conversation with her sister-in-law looks very much like an extract from some ballad that Jasim Uddin has puckishly slipped into the text. Doubtless the story had some connection with the scene about to take place. Note that the *kadam*, the tree of love, turns up here.

Vermilion? Here the stuff comes off in flakes;
I get no joy from wearing it.
Sunda and methi are no good
For rubbing on my body if they're pressed
In this locality; they make
Me sweat immediately they're on.'

'Lady, I've got the very things for you;
Ram Lakshman bangles[1] and the best
Vermilion China can produce;
It's only fitting for your face's charm.'
'And how much are they, if you please?
I want the truth, strange gipsy-man,[2]
No fobbing off, no fibs about the price.'

'If you would honour me this much,
To let me place them on your wrists,
I'll let you have the bangles free.
Grief forced me to take up this trade
And drag myself from place to place;
I don't need money. Let me dab your brow
With the vermilion, I'm content.
Favour thus far this landless man,
O lady of good fortune and respect.'

'I never heard of such a thing!
Sister-in-law, please tell this man

---

[1] Lakshman was Rama's devoted half-brother who accompanied him on his
wanderings and, according to Tulsi Das, was an incarnation of the serpent
king of the underworld. The bangles are probably made from the best conch
shells (the conch is sacred to Vishnu). They may be carved in the form of a
snake, or else be sold in pairs, one bigger than the other.

[2] The gipsy is referred to as a foreigner, and speaks of himself as wandering
from country to country (or district to district) even though he may be a
Bengali and never leave the province. This is because Bengal is divided into
many localities by waterway and jungle, and the people are of highly mixed
origin (comprising Mongolian, Aryan, Dravidian and Semitic stocks) whose
isolation quickly brings about significant differences in dialect, dress, and diet.
The situation is very much like that of nineteenth century Norway, or medieval
England or Germany. A Suffolk seaman came on shore in Kent in the time of
Chaucer and asked for 'egges'; the good-wife told him she was sorry but she
spoke no French. This enraged the seaman, who was as patriotic as the next
man. It was finally established that what he really wanted was 'eyren'.

To take his insolence away;
He ought to dress his own wife,
Not other people's, in these things.'
'O eyelash-coloured lady, no offence
Was meant; take none because I am
A foreigner. Pay what you think
Is fit, but let me put the bangles on.'

> 'You're a strange gipsy. In your boat
> You travel peddling everywhere.
> Why is it that your eyes are full of tears,
> Stooping to put these bangles on?
> You dab vermilion in my hair
> And weep at the same time. Sister-in-law,
> Withdraw a little while, please;
> I want to hear what he's got to say.'

'You are too beautiful to hear my tale;
Don't ask about it. Like the weeds
That drift by aimlessly, I go
My way. What good would come of telling you?
Father and mother, both are dead,
I have no friend to call my own;
I simply go about the land to trade,
And with me goes a broken heart.
You live contentedly; stay so.
Vermilion smiles between your parted hair,
And bracelets shine upon your wrists;
Love for your husband fills your heart.
Stay like this for me; live in happiness.'

> 'Who are you? Sojan? Is it you?
> Get out this minute, do you hear!
> Never come back again, never set foot
> Near Urankhali sandbank, not
> On purpose or by accident.
> I have forgotten everything,
> Who was Sojan, where or when.
> You never come into my thoughts,

Not even for one second, by mistake.
Take your bangles and your box
And never let your boat be seen
Along the Kumar river from tonight.'

'How is it possible to say
Such things? Open my heart and look,
Wound after welling wound swells to your gaze.
There's not the smallest corner left
A nail could do so much as scratch.'
'Much good that knowledge does me! Women seen
In conversation with strange men
Burn for a hundred years in Hell.
Get out, I say; get right away from here.
It's dead and buried now, don't drag
It out into the light of day;
Neighbours have prying eyes and walls have ears.
The world must hear no news of it;
Not a soul must ever know
That I had anything to do with you.'

 'No one will know, it's hidden deep
 Within the forest of my heart
 Beneath eternal mists, and kept alive
 On sorrow's dew. Only please wear
 These smiling gifts for me and I'll
 Go sailing down the river to my death.'
 'You only came in the belief
 I'd be unchaste. Do you expect
 I'd scandalize my husband's family line
 Accepting anything you give?'

'Oh, Duli! Duli! Strike me hard,
Strike hard and strike again; give me more pain.
Loose thunder on me from the sky,
Let my heart break, let my mind crack.
Father and mother, kindred, people, friends,
I left and thought no more of it,
All for your sake. Savage beasts

Were the companions in my search;
I went about my hidden task
As if I robbed a dead man's grave.
It was for love of you I took the rap
For all the guilt when I confessed
Before the judge. For seven years
I suffered unprotesting in that jail,
Mute as a bullock pressing oil;[1]
It wasn't easy, that I'll say.
If I served time it was for both of us.'

    'Go on, you're only saying that
    To soften me. But it's no good;
    My husband's name is higher than the sky
    So don't you come trying to blot
    His honour. I've forgotten all
    About our past affair. . . . But wait a bit,
    Now I remember that you gave
    Me anklets and a ring, once;
    I've kept them by me for some time,
    And since we happen to have met today
    I may as well give you them back.
    One other thing: I wove you a scarf
    Which now I'd like to be returned.
    If people saw my needlework
    They'd draw the wrong conclusions. Should you pass
    Along the Gauri where we built
    That little cottage I'd be glad
    If you'd go in to have a look
    If all those pictures of our life
    I painted on the walls remain;
    If so, you've got to wipe them all away
    In case they're seen, and someone spreads
    A false report. That's all behind;
    What is the use of living in the past?
    It was ignoble, I can't bear
    To call such squalid memories
    To mind. Let's not be sentimental now.'

[1] The bullock is driven in a circle turning the oil-press.

'Is this your final cruelty?
And is there no alternative
Now I am at my last extremity?
Relent and add some word besides.
If you've forgotten, you've done well;
What little that we shared brings me content.
Comfort me now before I'm snatched
Into the jaws of sombre death.
Did I come asking anything of you?
Yet you use thunder for your words.
Gods have no power to touch a man
Already stricken; can that man die twice?
My fate is written and I float
On sorrow's ocean for my deeds;
What pleasure do you gain from paining me?
Tell me what shameful deed of mine
Endangers you; and how your heart
Is satisfied setting dead wood alight.
Oh, Duli, Duli, must it be
This picture that I take away,
The hard and selfish bitch you have become?
I'll breathe my last upon the earth,
The soul will leave its cage behind
And spring into the void with beating wings;
How shall I spend the time till then
Now that I learn I've wasted life
In futile circling of a bitter lie?
Alas, alas, why did I come
Searching for you in gipsy dress;
Why did the stormy waves not sink my boat?
What was the use of finding you
If all it brings is further pain;
Why does my path stop short before death's pit?

Prophets and saints, where are you now?
Henceforth I give my heart to you;
Bless me so I forget this day's events.
Many are the mistakes I've made,
Today's no different from the rest;

Allow them to pass away as others have.
Now I'll forget as well as you
And guard no guilt in heart or mind;
Blot out the knowledge that I found you here,
Grant me this prayer, it's all I ask.
I'll raise my sail again, and point
The prow into the current's race.
I'll journey place to place once more,
From hythe to hythe I'll wander still,
Looking for Duli, only her.
The river's ribbon reaches to the sky,
One is alone upon its path,
And finds no resting places there.
Over the water's mirror I'll set sail,
A gipsy suffering the pangs
Of separation from his love;
I'll call the birds to me and ask
What golden province hides her house.
Why ever did I recognize your face?
Alas, alas, what have I found?
A slip, a little moment's slip
Poisons my whole existence till I die!'

'You're only thinking of yourself;
I've troubles of my own, you know.
But there's no need to tell you about that.
What is the use of digging up
Old clay? It's not worth crying once
The milk is spilt. But listen, you must go;
I hear my husband coming back.
Do not as much as hint we were
Acquainted once. Now bless me, if you can,
That I may wipe away the past
And with my husband's love forget
The history that you and I once shared.'

'Wait, wait, only turn round and look,
The forest that you set on fire
Still burns my soul as painfully.'

He flung himself upon the ground
And wept, but no one turned to wipe
His tears away. What perfumed sea
Could soothe away his searing wounds?

That burning pain is like the sun
Whose steaming breath scorches the noon.
It's burning, burns like the sand
Upon the incandescent plain
Of whirlwind-tortured Karbala.
It's burning, burns like a clap
Of thunder rending ghostly cloud.
It's burning, burns like the waves
Forced seething from the ocean's womb.
It's burning like volcanic pyres
That thrust up through the mountain's caves,
For ever burning as they surge.
And more than these, it burns, it burns,
Fanned by the sighs of fierce despair.
It burns as if a hundred flames
Swept wood and meadow in the wind;
With an infernal heat that burns
More fiercely than a hundred suns
It scalds but does not scorch the mind.
The burning heart still lives; it burns,
A living witness on the pyre;
Sighs like escaping gases burn.

All must be visited by fire:
Love's eagerness is burned, and caste
And creed; it burns the infant hope;
Ambition, aspiration, burn.
Wrapping itself round sleepless nights
Pain lurks in shadow, in the lap
Of endless dark and trackless void.
His heart's pyre spits a thousand flames,
Each blast a life-consuming breath.
Alas, what can extinguish it,
Whom could he tell, or who would help?

He walks alone whom anguish wastes
And he who weeps must want a friend.

Sojan picked up his useless tray,
With one last effort, walked away;
He walked straight on with dragging feet
And did not turn to look again,
His eyes, his face, rigid as flints.
The wood-path wound into the shade.

CHAPTER 21

Hard as a diamond, over the hills
The mountains lie whose sharpness cut
The golden necklace that I wear.

Brother, regard the market of beauty,
The myriad of colours playing;
Then look behind: fast falling is your day.

—Murshida song

Now John Henry had a little woman
And the dress that she wore was red,
But she started up the track
And, Lord! she never looked back,
'Goin' where John Henry lies dead,
Lord, lord,
Goin' where John Henry lies dead.'

—Traditional ballad

Unfolding the Jamdani sari from her box
    At nightfall, Duli dressed herself with care.
She painted sole and palm with lac, looked in the glass,
    Rubbed cheek and lip to redness, looked her best.
It seemed a streak of sun shone through her painted hair
    Where she had daubed a full vermilion line.
Wild flowers adorned her; bind-weed in her hair,
    On wrist and ankle ruffs of marigold.
'You look a farmer's queen dressed up in such attire,
    Bewitching, better still,' her husband said.

She pressed against him laughing roguishly; 'Not that,'
    She said. 'How can you lie so shamelessly?'
'Don't you believe me? Well, we'll call my brother in
    And ask him what he thinks. Let's have a bet.'
'You needn't bother; do you like me, tell the truth.'

170

'Better than treacle, more than jilabi;[1]
How can I put it better? As the harrow bites
    Into the field, as paddy shoots are bound
In bundles, so my soul is linked in yours with joy.
    It pleases me far more than Gazi songs.
You are a pumpkin flower and I the bumble-bee.'

            'Well just suppose that someone tried
                To carry me away tonight
                By force; what would you do?'

            'What is this nonsense, dear?
                It isn't possible;
All of the village knows you are my wife.
                We married legally,
                That's common knowledge here,
I haven't stolen you from anyone.
                And even if some chap
                Came round here claiming you,
Why should you run away with him? I am
                Your husband, after all.
                Oh well, girls will be girls,
You must be humoured in your little jokes.'

            'But just suppose that someone came
                And took me off; what would you do?
                I want to know right now.'

            'What's that? Gora-chand Rai,
                Grandson of Dharam Chad,
Could stun an elephant with one hard slap.[2]
                As long as I'm alive,
                Kala Chad Rai, his son,
No man would dare to snatch my wife away.
                I'd break his bones to bits,

[1] *Jilabi* is a sweetmeat made from batter squeezed in thin circles in hot fat
and then dipped in syrup.
[2] Rai ancestry: to have a strong man as an ancestor is a very proud boast.
Confidence in this knowledge makes a man give of his best and, at the same
time, causes others to be wary of offending him.

I'd split him like a bean,
I'd knock his block off with one finger-flick.
    Well, now you know. That's fine.
    Sit down and let me part
Your hair; just bend your neck a little more.
    And it's my turn to ask
    You something now. What put
It in your head to get dressed up like this?'

    'I see you don't approve;
    Then I'll remove it all.'

'Now don't get angry; I'm just ignorant.
    Try to put up with me;
    I haven't got the gift
Of putting words to what I really mean.
    You brighten up the house
    No end when you get dressed
Like that, to tell the truth. But I'm not rich
    Enough for you to have
    The clothes that you deserve,
Brilliant with rich and splendid ornaments.
    The little that I bring
    You pout at and won't wear.
It grieves me constantly that this straw hut
    Holds Laksmi prisoner,
    A hovel for a queen,
And I offend the heavens all my life.
    But fortune smiles today,
    My Duli sits content
Her wretched husband worships at her feet.
    I'll tell you what I feel
    Seeing you dressed so well:
I wish that you could dress thus every day;
    It suits you to the ground,
    And when I look at you
I want to dance around and sing out loud.

    'People could husk their rice

In that big mouth of yours
If you weren't always opening it to yap!'

'You'd be a gonner then; I'd chomp
You into flattened smithereens.
        Oh well, that's over with.
        I hear the gipsies came
        In strength a while ago;
Why didn't you buy anything to wear?
        Just listen to that flute
        Playing from one of their boats;
Ho-hum, now there's heart-rending sound for you.'

'Bah, ashes to the flute! I want
To have some fun; let's yarn the night
        Away and have a laugh.'

'Now just shut-up a bit;
I never heard such sound
So sweet before; I'd like to be the bird
        Buoyed up by such a tune.'

'Will you listen to me!
Go over there and tell the man to stop.'

'Now why should I do that?
What's wrong with it? It's like
Pain flying in the night, a wind that speaks
        The language of the heart.
        Listen, bend back you ears.'

'Well I don't like it; get it stopped at once.
        You brag and boast in vain,
        "I can do this and that",
And you can't even stop a little noise!'

'I'm sleepy; just keep quiet.
I think it is the flute
That lies upon my eyelids like lead weights.'

'Not that, you mustn't sleep tonight.
Out in the murky depths of dark
        Along black misty paths
Where star-lamps swing, that cruel flute
Is playing on the troubled wind
        And fashions someone's noose
Upon its swaying thread of tune.
Oh, husband, why must you sleep now?
        Lord of my body's love,
Subject my hapless heart to yours
With kisses and your gentle hands;
        Bind me to you for life.
Wake up, a subtle thief has come
To steal all that is dear to you.
        But no, I'll never make
My husband's place unclean with thoughts
Of someone else. I'm not like that.
        Clear out of here, rude sound!'

Cruel flute, along what secret paths do you invade
        The heart? She stops her ears, she shuts the door,
She tears a corner from her sari to stuff tight
        The holes about the wall.[1] But that cruel flute
Would not obey her orders to stay out, it forced
        Her to remember wealth and property
And husband's name to steel herself. All floats away,
        Alas, before the current of that flute.
Where should the helpless girl find strength? Tune floods on
            tune
        A thousand-fold, encroaching every way
At once, awakening old memories of night;
        Event upon event wound round with sound
Rose to the surface like dark serpents from the swamp.

It cannot be! What can a woman do?

[1] Shutting out the flute: there is, here, an allusion to the story of Radha and
Krishna. She refused to see him in a fit of jealousy over his dallying with other
cow-herd girls. When he plays his flute on the banks of the river Jumna she
attempts at first to shut out the sound but in the end relents and goes out to
join him in the night.

Her heart's the culture's puppet, she its prisoner.
And still the flute plays: 'cruel woman, for what guilt
        Did you throw me out and kill me with that blow?
        What guilt made you forget me? If it's true,
What joy have you in pummelling harsh words on me?
I cannot bear it.' Still the flute plays, every note
        Laces the wind and sews the sky with pain.

'Wake, husband, wake, and say goodbye for ever; dawn
        Will see you robbed of this unlucky girl.
        Be witness sun and moon, and all you gods,
Have you not heard the weeping of unhappiness?
Vermilion in my hair, be witness that the flute
        Calls me to put the noose about my neck.
I'm going, oh unlucky husband, through no fault
        Of yours, but with fate's writing on my brow,
        Fulfilling destiny. You'll weep for me
Tomorrow morning, you'll go mad to no avail.
The thought of it will stay with me after I'm dead.
        Our first six months I would not speak a word,
        Another six I brooded on my grief.
You went such lengths to make me happy every day,
I never gave you happiness in all my life.
        Forgive me now, forgive my poison heart
        Whose acid burns whoever I have touched.
Be witness, dark of night, wearing the garb of stars,
And mother earth be witness on the serpent's head;[1]
        Tonight I'm leaving with a broken heart,
        Yours be whatever happiness is left.'
And still the flute plays by the sandbank in the dark.
The careless wind falls to the earth with broken wings.

Slowly, then, very slowly, bending at his feet
        She leaves him one last greeting smudged in red.
Then carefully, so carefully and slow, so soft
        And soundlessly, she steals out of the door,
Rushes through fields, tearing the darkness with both hands.
        And still the flute plays: 'Duli, you forgive

[1] On a serpent's head the earth is borne, according to Hindu mythology.

All of whatever guilt of mine remains:
If I have brought my pain into your happy house,
If awkwardness has come from my remembering you.
      But you forgive me since I've borne the weight
Of sorrows manifold upon all compass points.'

  'Oh, Sojan, Sojan, must you bear such grief
When my request was to forget this luckless one?'

        'Who is it? Who are you?
    Ah, Duli, Duli, have you come
    To stir the fire you set alight?
        Never was grief such weight!
    You need not fear me any more,
    No one will come reminding you
        Again of days gone by;
    None will destroy your husband's pride.
    But since you've come stand in my sight
        And let your beauty mist
    My eyes, here at life's terminus.
    All change, all changes, let me keep
        One changeless memory.'

  'What are you saying, Sojan? Why
    Do you fill your golden life with grief
        Remembering a girl
    Not worth the trouble? Go back home,
    Make inquiries, start afresh,
        Marry and settle down.'
  'Duli, I fall before your feet;
    Have pity on me, do not pierce
        My heart with further pain.'

  'Listen, I've got it all worked out.
    If both of us remain alive
        Neither is safe any more.
    I would be easy to forget
    If I were dead, and I'd be glad
        To die for such a cause.

Men cannot understand how hard
It is when women give their heart
     Away and then are forced
To take as husband someone else.
I've battled with myself, but now
     My strength has given out
And I no longer wish to live.
But there is something you must know
     Now that pretence is vain.
Forget that Duli that you met
Today; there is another one
     Besides, whose every breath
Was drawn in sorrow at her loss,
At separation from her love,
     In loveless solitude.'

'Repeat those words; they are enough
To make the dead desire to live;
     I can't believe it!'
'Sojan, you're everything to me,
Except for you I recognize
     No living being else.
You are my inner world of calm content,
You are the outer shell surrounding me,
Enthral me body, soul and mind.'

'Alas, alas, you should have said
Before, and then I would have borne
     A few days more of life.
But as it is, you come too late;
Death's ferry moors close into shore.
     I've taken poison.'

'What's that? Unsay it! Oh, my love,
     Have I done this to you?
If you must go, take me as well;
We'll quit this meagre hamlet, earth,
     This mired and blotchy earth,

This ill-baked tile; be witness sun,
Moon, stars, and gods, how we escape
This trap of misery.'

Dawn the unmerciful, that does not care who wakes
Unwillingly, that forces on the sight
Of teeming earth, metropolis of misery,
Hardship and cruelty, disease and death,
And does not deign to look away with downcast eyes
As others do, but turns its blazing orb
Unwavering on all as if they were not there,
Spied out the sandbank, stirred along the forms
Of gipsy youth and village maiden clasped and close,
Limb touching limb, arm loosely cradling neck,
And it was not abashed to call the curious
To pry and spy and cast up arm and eye.
Too late. Their souls had kicked aside the golden door;
There is no shame about an empty cage.

CHAPTER 22

O bring the boat, the boat to the hythe,
And bring the boat to shore,
For I must seek the merchant,
I have great business there,
And bring the boat to hythe.

I sailed this boat from wharf to wharf
But I could find no shore,
And in this river set afloat
My golden-coloured flower,
And bring my boat to hythe.

—Murshida song[1]

O shall I leap in the river
And knock upon Paradise door
For a gunner of twenty seven and a half
And a queen of twenty four?
From the almond tree by the river
I watch the sky with a groan
For Jumper and Kate are always out late
And I lie here alone.

—'Ballad of Katherine of Aragon', Charles Causley

Daytime was dead; evening[2] prepared herself
To mount the pyre, bathed at the riverside,
Scribbled vermilion on her brow and wrapped
Her body in the silken cloth of clouds.
The curving surface of the earth is lined

---

[1] A *Murshida* song is a kind of sustained religious allegory. In this the boat and the golden flower stand for the body, not finding shore is to be in a frustrated emotional state, the market-place is the world in which we carry on our commerce with life and in which the merchant is Allah. It represents, therefore, a longing for fulfilment, possibly through death.

[2] Evening, the day's wife, is preparing herself for *suttee*, self-immolation, an old Hindu custom which the British did their best to stamp out.

With light and weeps at the touch of her bright feet.
Slowly she steps and balances the moon
Upon her head; the Great Bear's seven saints[1]
Read charms from the far canopy of sky.
Behind her come her mourning friends, the stars,
Ready to follow her into the pyre;
The crickets chorus and they blink back tears.
The tributary river's country stream
Carries its sorrows past the village quays;
Small ripples lap the breast-work of the banks
And tell its story with melodious tears.

Whose boat is sailing down this eerie tide
Filling the minstrel wind with a kindred grief?
He steers his craft along its winding path
      Hailing and asking all, 'How far is it
      To what is known as Sojan the Gipsy's wharf?'
      'What Sojan do you mean? Where does he live?'
      'Ah listen, listen to that sad story,
      Listen, listen to that unhappy tale.'
With this he fastens to his boat and sings;
The wailing sarinda accompanies
The ebb-tide tune, the bhatiali song.

      'In Simul Toli underneath the trees,
      Sojan and Duli's playground, it befell.
      Listen, listen, no story can compare:
      Leaving their people, leaving their friends,
      Two lovers went embracing in deep night;
      They built a cottage on the Gauri's bank,
      Beneath its shade they rocked their mutual dreams.
      A stormy night has felled that cottage now,
      And Duli marries in another place.
      Then listen, people, to the gipsy's tale:
      Life's lamp is out, their love can never die;

[1] Seven saints (*rishis* or seers such as are said to have written the *Veda*, an early collection of hymns which make up yet another section of the Hindu scriptures) who are stellified in the constellation of the Great Bear.

Even today they weep in solitude,
Clasped in the shade of some village landing-place.'

The song is finished, people wipe their eyes,
    Ask, 'Where did you hear that? Who told it you?'
    'I heard it on my travels from the lips
    Of various folk, but I know nothing more.
    River by river I've sailed in search
    Of that wharf. There, I've heard, all who feel the pain
    Of separation find relief at night,
    Heart's sorrow cools in all who reach that place.
    The women fill their pitchers there and shed
    A tear for them before returning home.'
    'O brother boatman, should you find that place
    Bring us a little pilgrim water back.'

Into the distance down the water's path
The boatman sails; the evening star goes out,
And all the western sky is blue with night.

APPENDIX I

GRAVES[1]

Here, under the pomegranate tree, is your grandmother's grave;
For thirty years my tears have kept it green.
She was a little doll-faced girl when she came to my home,
And she wept to be done with the play of her childhood days.

Returned from my travelling once, I suddenly knew
She had been in my thoughts all the time.
Like the dawn her golden face would blind my eyes,
And from that day I lost myself among small joys of hers.

There along that path I'd take the plough to the fields
And, leaving, would turn
For a last look at her to take with me.
How she'd smile, my long-wed sister-in-law, because of this!

When she went to her father's house she said, touching my feet,
'Do not forget to visit me soon at the village of Ujan-toli.'
So when I sold melons at market I saved a few coins
And bought her a necklace of beads, tobacco and toothpowder.
(And what's so funny in that, my lad?)

How happy your grandmother was when she got these small gifts;
If only you could have seen her fingering her nose-ring.
She said, 'You have come after so many days;
I have been waiting in tears,
Watching the path for you,' smiling now.

When we parted for a mere few days you couldn't console her;
I wonder how she sleeps in her grave in this lonely place?
Fold your hands, grandson, and pray:
'Come, oh merciful God,
Let Paradise descend for my grandmother.'

Empty the life I endured when she left me;

[1] See page 24. Original title '*Kobor*', first published in 1929 in *Rakhali*
(Pastoral Poems).

Yet it seems each one I embraced here has gone,
Following her to that distant land.
A hundred graves are carved on the stone of my heart;
I get confused counting the number, computing it over and over
        again.

These wrinkled hands that hold the spade
Have buried so many beloved faces under hard earth
That I have come to love it, press it to my heart.
Come, kneel and pray, grandson;
Perhaps tears will relieve this pain.

Here sleeps your father, and here your mother sleeps:
Still your tears, while I tell you their story.

One April morning my boy called out,
'Father, I cannot go to the fields today.'
I spread out a mat on the floor for him, said 'Sleep, my Son.'
How could I know that this would be his last slumber?

A clean coffin I made him, and as I carried him here
'Where are you taking my father?' you followed crying.
I could not answer, my little son,
All the words in the world turned away grieving.

Night and day your mother's tears were unceasing,
Clasping your father's yoke and plough in both hands.

For sorrow the leaves fell from the forest trees,
The winds of April wailed in the empty rice-fields;
And villagers passing along that path wiped their eyes.
Even the leaves they trod underfoot crumpled and died.

From their stall the two bullocks regarded the unploughed fields
While your mother clung to their necks with heart-broken sobs
Till it seemed the whole village would drown
In oceans of her weeping.

Perhaps the tears of that lovely girl
Found a path to the land of the dead.
In the morning of her life she longed for evening;
Ah, poor girl, she wove her own shroud with her hands.

Before her death she summoned you to her:
My child, she said, my greatest pain is
Leaving you motherless in this world,
My darling, my jewel, my son.
What blessings she gave you!

Then to me, 'Over my grave hang my husband's wide wicker
        sun-hat;
It will swing in the wind.'
Long ago that hat fell and mixed with the dust.
But the pain in my heart still cries out
For these two that sleep in the shade.

How lovingly the tree-boughs bend above;
The fire-fly maidens of evening light lamps
And the crickets make music with small bells tinkling.
Fold your hands, grandson and pray: 'O come, eternal God,
Let Paradise descend now for father and mother.'

Here is that fair little maiden, your sister's grave.
We gave her in marriage to a high-caste merchant's family;
They did not love such a darling girl, they punished her,
Not with blows, but more cruelly, with words.

Message on message she sent me:
Grandfather, come tomorrow,
Take me to the land of my people
For one or two days.

The heartless father-in-law let her come one winter at last;
Her face was pale, a smile no longer bloomed there.
Some days she passed by her parents' grave
Till death's flute called her away, and here I made her grave.

See how softly the grass and forest flowers caress her;
The wild doves sing her litany.
Fold your hands, grandson, and pray:
'Let Paradise descend for my unloved sister.'

Here lies my youngest child of seven years,
A brilliant rainbow bursting the gates of Paradise open.

Who knows what her thoughts were
Losing her mother so young?
When I looked in her face
Your grandmother came to my mind,
And I clasped her to me
While tears washed the colour from the sky.

Returning from market one day
I found her stretched out in the dust
As if she had fallen asleep,
Hugging her doll, tired of play.
The black cobra that bit her
Had slithered away in the bush.

How bitter my tears were, laying my darling to bed in the grave.
Go soft, do not speak, little grandson, lest we wake her.
Slowly, dig slowly, slowly, let me see
How my heaven on earth lies sleeping
Under the black-baked bitter soil.

The warm-coloured sunset has kissed the fields
And great is my desire to hug the earth around me close today.
The call to prayer floats from the mosque;
Let us fold our hands, little grandson, and pray:
'O come, eternal God, let Paradise descend for our loved ones.'

APPENDIX 2

On Translation, and on translating Jasim Uddin

To embark upon translation is immediately to come face to face with a crisis of conscience. Either one intends to take the scholarly approach of being absolutely faithful to the text, or else one means to be faithful to the spirit of the work. This latter is the one I have favoured for this work, and I am guiltily conscious of how wide a field of potential error lies therein. Faced with an Eastern text to be interpreted for Western eyes, the problem is increased, especially since my job has been to impose literary form at second hand. I have been greatly indebted to Mrs Painter for the very thorough job she has made of reducing the Bengali to English with a wealth of annotation, and am loath to have her blamed for what some may take as cavalier attitudes on my part. For my objective has been to please the general reader, to make a living work of a verse-novel whose themes are vital to the understanding of the peoples of the Indian subcontinent and, especially at these times, to the cause of peace. Such themes should take us beyond the little questions of grammatical equivalent and exact synonym.

Though my maxim is that 'the letter killeth but the spirit giveth life' I am well aware that this does not mean, and never has, that you make the thing up as you go along with a scornful glance at the text now and then. But it does mean that if a poem is good, and *Sojan Badiar Ghat* is very good, it deserves to read well in a translation. It deserves to read like a poem and not a patent word for word transmogrification. The word 'poet', by its derivation, means somebody who *makes* something; similarly the word 'poem' means that which is made, the artefact. The translator of a poem, then, does not merely disassemble and then reassemble, as though he were handling a motor-cycle engine; he must *remake*. Ben Jonson, writing on 'imitation', the third requisite of a poet (or maker) defines it as 'not to imitate servilely, as Horace saith, and catch at vices, for vertue: but to draw forth out of the best and choicest flowers, with the Bee, and turne all into Honey'. As it is, one dimly sees in too many translations the richness of the original, but is prevented from giving in to it fully because of the dough-like interpretation. There is nothing worse than a tear forming at the eye that will not fall, or a cry of admiration that turns to a cough in the throat. If, then, for the sake of euphony or rhythm a minor amount of inexactitude should arise; if some of the lines are rearranged to avoid hiatus, repetition, or obscurity; and if, in order to avoid banality or mystification, wording not in the original is substituted, one should welcome the foreign bodies as part of the maker/translator's duties.

Why this should be so, especially in as large a work as the present, ought not to need stating. For the sake of others who hold different views, equally strong and sincere, however, it must be. The problem centres around what it is most important to conserve in translation. We have recently seen it assume the proportions of a minor scholarly battle over interpretations of Boris Pasternak's poems. His sister takes up the antagonistic position in the preface to her translations:

'It is almost impossible to produce a perfect English poem while at the same time preserving the Russian flavour, the content, the melody and rhythm of the original as well as the personality of the poet; one has to sacrifice at least one of these qualities in order to be free to manipulate the others more or less successfully. Individual translators sacrifice different things, according to what seems to them most important to preserve. For my part . . . I believe that a translation from Pasternak must *sound* like the original, and though I try to produce an acceptable English poem I do not think that this is the most important of my tasks.' (*Poems*, trans. Lydia Pasternak Slater. Peter Russel)

The opposite view is taken by A. Alvarez in a review of Donald Davie's *The Poems of Dr Zhivago*. He quotes a passage from one of Davie's translations which, while admitting it 'may be more literal, more accurate and closer to dictionary Russian' than a freer version by Max Hayward and Manya Harari, he finds no improvement on it. He goes on to comment *à propos* of their translation:

'Perhaps this loses some of Pasternak's subtlety and movement, but it certainly seems to me clearer, less finicky, mannered and involuted than Prof. Davie's version. I would also have thought its language closer to the simplicity Pasternak apparently aims for in his later work. Only three of Davie's versions . . . have an edge on the original translations, and with those he rather shame-facedly admits to have taken liberties. If only he had taken a few more.' (*Observer*, 12.x.65)

At the same time as Alvarez was thus arguing I discussed my attitude to the present work with another translator who took the extreme view that 'unless the rhythm, syllabic pattern, rhyme-scheme, alliteration and the lot are preserved in a translation, then it is not perfect'. I trust I may be indulged in quoting my correspondence in reply: 'I tend to sympathize with your rigorous standards for translation, so far as lyrics go. You could hardly do that for a full-scale work—*Paradise Lost*, for example. One would soon descend to gibberish, it would take too long, be too obscure, and drive you mad. Another thing is that you stress faithfulness to technique and skate airily over reproducing the meaning; not just word for word, but what the poet is trying to say. That is at least as important as technique. So also is producing a satisfying English poem, not just a caricature of the original which, in English, would seem alien, stale, or banal. If one is going to concentrate on the *feel* of the original then the resultant search for good words and right words is going to interfere awfully with your technique. True, with immense pains, which means a very slow rate of progress, the perfect cameo can be produced; but then the slightest small flaw ruins the whole.' Perhaps my attitude is best summed up in the words of the Tudor, Sir Thomas North, himself quoting the French Amyot: 'The office of a fit translator consisteth not only in the faithful expressing of his author's meaning, but also in a certain resembling and shadowing forth of the form of his style and manner of his speaking.'

In translating Jasim Uddin I have tried to make such theorizing over into fact. I am well aware that with most theorizing poets the promise is not often lived up to, but that mercifully they often break their own rules. I do not think that I am an exception; I can only tabulate some of my working methods.

Bengali literature is full of conventions which Western literature has been in the process of shaking off for a century or more. The verse technique is intricate and there are very many rhetorical tropes. Some correspond to those of the West, and are very effective even if they are seldom used now. Others are not allowed for in our vast canon of 'poetic licence', and would merely puzzle, annoy, or amuse, if followed too faithfully. For instance, anyone rushing out to deeds of 'derring-do' is usually in the habit of rending the welkin with his shouts. After the skies have toppled down with alarming persistence half a dozen times or so, and one is still nowhere in sight of the end, the novelty tends to pall. Either one ignores it hereafter, or one stretches one's ingenuity to find something cognate but requiring different wording for these cries, shouts, roars and yells to do. It still happens enough times to adopt both approaches. I suspect there are rather more ways of putting it in Bengali. And this is just one example out of many.

From the point of view of sounds, syllabic patterns, assonance, and alliteration, it is obviously not always possible for them to be reproduced exactly where they occur in the original. But one may compensate for this where the English wording permits it elsewhere. Getting the feel of the poem is what matters most. Where there is a pun in the text, however, I have done my best to match it, though naturally not as well. Again, with the proviso that no violence be done to the work, I have indulged in word-play elsewhere.

Hardest to interpret for a Westerner are those passages in the poem dealing with specifically Eastern things. True, one may have recourse to the notes, but for every strange occurrence to be glossed would be tedious, as well as breaking the reader's concentration. I have, therefore, occasionally incorporated the gloss into the poem. Minor examples would be adding the word 'tree' where the author only mentions its proper name, or mentioning the colour of a berry or fruit when it does not occur in the original. But it must be pointed out that Jasim Uddin is often anything but reticent in his descriptions, calling up colours, shapes, and movement readily and skilfully. On the other hand, though the author is very explicit on the ceremonies and beliefs of his own religion (Islam), Hindu customs and thinking, which appear almost as frequently, are treated with far less, if any, detail. Granted the Muslim likes nothing better than to be told and retold about his religion, and not to be reminded too forcefully that there are others; a reader in the 'Christian' West needs to know as much as possible about everything that occurs. Rather than that the notes should assume the proportions of a minor sociological tract I have sometimes added a minimum gloss where it is necessary for the reader's immediate understanding.

Most impossible to deal with are literary and other allusions, and half quotations, incorporated into the text. Jasim Uddin himself is reticent upon this subject, but it is an acknowledged part of his poetic method. It would be useless even to hint at what is going on; nor can Western translators be expected to gather every instance of it. Here again what might be called the law of *mutatis mutandis* comes into operation. It often happens that the wording of the original happens to coincide with some passage well known to the Westerner. At the beginning of Chapter 6, in the passage referring to the activities of Nayeb's judicial pen,

occurs a line roughly translatable as: 'With one of its strokes
many huts have lost their thatch-coverings.' Now this, especially
insofar as it relates to the eventual fate of Simul Toli village, is
reminiscent of Dylan Thomas' 'The hand that signed the paper
felled a city'. I have accordingly reproduced the line thus:

> The hand that wields that pen can fell a town:
> One stroke and all the houses lose their thatch.

Another example occurs in Chapter 19, where Duli wonders whom
her love has injured that she (by Karmic process) should be made
to feel like injuries from it. In doing so she comes near to voicing
Donne's question in *The Canonization:*

> Alas, alas, who's injur'd by my love?

The most obvious adaptation in the cause of Western understanding is in the epigraphs where, as well as preserving the
originals, I have also provided Western near-equivalents so that
the reader might respond to them, and gain some hint of what is
to follow in the accompanying chapter, in the same way as does
the Bengali.

I have tried to reproduce as far as possible the mannerisms of
speech of the various people in the poem, especially in so far as it
gives an indication of their character, or the emotions they are
experiencing. Jasim Uddin does a lot of subtle characterization
this way, and at least half the poem consists of dialogue. But I hope
that I have shown moderation. Jasim Uddin makes great use of
the Bengali peasant dialect, at which I can only hint by using
colloquial rhythms and the occasional colloquialism. There is
nothing I hate more than incompetent attempts to reproduce
spoken dialect. The only really effective use of this in translation/
adaptation that I can call to mind is in Dudley Fitts' admirable
versions of Aristophanes' plays. I cannot hope to equal him, and
would hesitate to assign any equivalent which might suggest the
speech of an Indian peasant. The best one can do in such a case
is try to match idiom for idiom, proverb for proverb. I found this
surprisingly easy in some cases because they are very similar in
both languages; 'Keep your hair on', for example. One or two
rhetorical flourishes match as well. Chapter 15 begins with the
story-teller's conventional appeal for attention on the part of his
audience; there is a similar example in Chapter 22. This sort of

beginning was popular in fifteenth-century England, and I have translated it accordingly.

Particular thought was given to the choice of verse-forms, since here I had to diverge widely from usage in the original. The standard measure for Bengali narrative poetry seems to be seven-footed trochaic rhymed couplets. Rhyming translations too often force one to twist the meaning of the lines unjustifiably, as well as being a temptation to do the syntax violence. That is the sort of temptation it is a positive pleasure to resist. Trochaic measure was also out of the question; it is virtually impossible to use it without sounding like *Hiawatha*. Nor did I intend using the unwieldy fourteener line; the Earl of Surrey was one of the few poets ever to use that measure at all successfully, and only then after considerable trial and error. Apart from its appearance in Tudor times, its most common form is split into ballad-measure, one totally inappropriate for *Sojan Badiar Ghat*. No, one must use the equivalent English narrative line, the iambic pentameter. It works out very roughly as four Bengali lines equalling five or six English lines. Having established that trochaic heptameter couplets are equivalent to blank verse in iambic pentameter, I proceeded thereafter by adding or subtracting a syllable wherever two are added or subtracted in the Bengali line. The four basic measures may be expressed thus:

1. Bengali heptameter.
   English pentameter in the ratio 4:5/6.

2. Bengali octameter.
   English 22 syllable two-lined unit, divided 12, 10.

3. Bengali hexameter.
   English 18 syllable two-lined unit, divided 10, 8.

4. Bengali pentameter.
   English octosyllabics (with variations).

There are exceptions. In a more lyrical (as opposed to narrative) context I prefer lines to be shorter, and have therefore varied section 2 thus:

2a. English 22 syllable three-lined unit, divided 8, 8, 6.

2b. English 22 syllable three-lined unit, divided 6, 6, 10.

The former of these is a good medieval measure; the latter is lighter, more Elizabethan, lacking the dying fall of the other. The two clash together in the conversation between Duli and her husband in Chapter 21. I did not wish to rely on octosyllabics throughout Sojan and Duli's quarrelling in Chapter 20. The measure is too lightweight and needs reinforcing with pentameters now and then. It gives the jerky trouble effect of the argument. The standard measure here was a three-lined unit, divided 8, 8, 10. But I preferred not to be too strict about the form and simply let myself be guided by the exigencies of the wording.

It is evident that mine is not a scholarly translation, and that scrupulous literal accuracy has been sacrificed for the sake of attempting a readable English poem with the feel of the original. I have, however, let myself be guided by others as to how far I might diverge. If my methods are to be placed, they are on the borderline of 'creative translation' as defined by J. P. Sullivan in his study *Ezra Pound & Sextus Propertius* (Faber, 1964). Certainly *Gipsy Wharf* does not aspire to be the equal of Pound's 'Homage to Sextus Propertius' any more than that poem compares with Johnson's 'London'. But it bows in the direction of a tradition which is not confined to Europe. There are Indian, indeed Bengali, precedents for creative translation of great latitude. The original Sanskrit *Ramayana*, an epic dealing with Rama's life written by Valmiki about 400 B.C., was later translated into both Hindi and Bengali. It received a considerable amount of rehandling in the process, for Rama had been elevated from legendary hero to avatar of Vishnu since the writing of the original, and this was reflected in the text.

Tulsi Das was responsible for the Hindi version in 1532. A few years later the English poet, Sir Thomas Wyatt, undertook a similar kind of translation/paraphrase of the Penitential Psalms. In this we find him adapting the stylistic parallelism of the Hebrew to English verse, and filling out the original with explanation of allusions and underlining the psalmist's meaning; in addition he expands certain images and adds others of his own making (or incorporates them from contemporary commentaries), without departing from the spirit of the text. Another similarity, parallel to the shift from heroic to divine in the treatment of Rama, is Wyatt's changing the traditional Catholic emphasis on penance for sin, apparent in former treatments, to that of the Lutheran penitence and forgiveness through faith. Nearer to our own time is Fitzgerald's extraordinary *Omar Khayyam* in all four of its recensions. In fact, as Sullivan points out, insistence on faithfulness to the original is comparatively recent: 'It is a canon of romantic criticism to stress the undefiled original impulse; it is not a classical canon'.

On the other hand, we cannot afford to ignore the new canon now it is with us. It gives rise to the valid comment that it ought to be the personality and style of the original author that comes through in a translation, and not those of the translator; and that to interpret is to impose something of oneself upon the poem. But then a certain amount of intrusion is unavoidable, especially if one is writing in a widely separated language. (Bengali and English *do* have a common origin in Indo-European and there remain, even now, certain similarities.) In addition, each man has his own style which it is impossible to subordinate entirely. But if, as I have stressed repeatedly, one's aim is to preserve the feel of the original, then the risk is minimized.

One is not, for instance, updating ancient allusions, as was Johnson in 'London' and 'The Vanity of Human Wishes', both based on satires by Juvenal. Nor is one making the elegant additions with which Chapman bejewelled his translation of Homer. And notice that it is 'Chapman's Homer', not Homer in Chapman's translation, or the Chapman version. There have been other versions more famous for their translator's felicity than for their faithfulness: Golding's Ovid, Dryden's Virgil, Pope's Homer. In each of these it is the interpreter's personal style, his additions to and adaptations of the original that interest us. This is not to say that they were not sincerely trying to interpret what they took to be the spirit of their authors. Dryden and Pope believed their heroic couplets contained within them the essence of classical decorum, and so strong was their persuasion that many still believe this; but there are many more now who do not. There is nothing like a heroic couplet in Homer, and Virgil's versification is more dissimilar than similar. But they spoke for their age, and in the age's language, and therefore were accepted by it. For this reason Eliot and Pound have insisted that a translation, if it is to be acceptable as literature, cannot but be an echo of the age's voice and hold up the mirror to it. There can, therefore, be no final rendering since viewpoints differ and voices change with time. In fact, there can be no translation (as transliteration), only recreation. Translation is a technique for making **dead** poets *alive now*, for making foreign tongues express what we would say were we there.

But the reason why these authors of translations, largely of classical poets, could afford to diverge from their texts is obvious. The majority of their readers could understand the original anyway. What they required was a presentable English poem based on the text they admired. Also the author was dead; he could neither be consulted nor protest. In the case of *Sojan Badiar Ghat* its author is still very much alive, and any extratextual enthusiasms must be curbed in deference to him. His work is not a religious or philosophical text requiring interpretation, and there is no question of changing his emphases. And although it touches upon Eastern themes requiring a limited amount of amplification in order to be fully understood by the reader, many of us are aware of the deeper problems with which it deals.

One may sum up by pointing out the weak points in both of the main forms of translation. These forms are, in the words of Guy Davenport, either 'a methodical transposition of lexico-graphic equivalents, or a remaking, from scratch as it were, of a verbal structure to contain an emotion or idea . . . that informs the words of the original'. (*Poetry*, January 1966, p. 264.) To hold entirely to the former scholarly approach is to produce something appealing ultimately only to scholars. To take the latter and try to produce an equivalent work of art is to remain within the realm of human fallibility. How wide is expressed by J. P. Sullivan: 'An almost infinite series of changes are made in phrasing, feeling, tone, nuance, ornament and form. Some correspond merely to the different structure or vocabulary of the languages involved, but other changes may be far more radical and deliberate, and will be made according to the translator's principles, the purpose of the translation, the resources of the two languages, and the sensibilities of the original writer and his translator.' Since translations are made with materials that are constantly in a state of flux they have to be remade constantly, either because previous attempts seem to fall below the original, or else they go beyond it and live an independent life of their own. If authors themselves are often dissatisfied with their work and rewrite it, or as one might say, retranslate their thoughts into different words and forms, how much less ultimately satisfactory can be a translation from one language to another, and from one culture into another.

YANN LOVELOCK

June 1967, Sheffield.

GEORGE ALLEN & UNWIN LTD

Head Office
40 Museum Street, London, W.C.1
Telephone: 01-405 8775

Sales, Distribution and Accounts Departments
Park Lane, Hemel Hempstead, Herts.
Telephone: 0442 3244

Athens: 34 Panepistimiou Street
Auckland: P.O. Box 36013, Northcote Central N.4
Barbados: P.O. Box 222, Bridgetown
Bombay: 103–105 Fort Street, Bombay 1
Beirut: Deeb Building, Jeanne d'Arc Street
Calcutta: 285J Bepin Behari Ganguli Street, Calcutta 12
Cape Town: 68 Shortmarket Street
Hong Kong: 105 Wing On Mansion, 26 Hancow Road, Kowloon
Ibadan: P.O. Box 62
Karachi: Karachi Chambers, Mcleod Road
Madras: 2/18 Mount Road, Madras
Mexico: Villalongin 32, Mexico 5, D.F.
Nairobi: P.O. Box 30583
Philippines: P.O. Box 157, Quezon City D-502
Rio de Janeiro: Caixa Postal 2537-Zc-00
Singapore: 36c Prinsep Street, Singapore 7
Sydney N.S.W.: Bradbury House, 55 York Street
Tokyo: C.P.O. Box 1728, Tokyo 100–91
Toronto: 81 Curlew Drive, Don Mills

BIBHUTIBHUSHAN BANERJI

PATHER PANCHALI

Bibhutibhushan Banerji's remarkable masterpiece, is acknowledged as one of the greatest Bengali novels ever written. Popular throughout the length and breadth of India, the story has already been brought to audiences in Europe and America by the widely acclaimed film directed by Satyajit Ray. Now for the first time the novel itself is available in English.

Pather Panchali is a vivid, moving and authentic portrayal of the life of a Brahmin household seen through the eyes of the two young children of the family, Opu and his elder sister Durga. Few authors in any literature can rival Banerji's understanding of the child mind. He writes of Opu and Durga and their friends, at home or out at play, with a natural realism unmarred by adult condescension. We can hear and see them; we go with them where every impulse leads and take part in all they do and feel. So too, we get to know every inch of the village and all its people; its houses, fields and paths; its trees, fruits and flowers; the river, the pools where the children love to play; the tangled undergrowth where they can get away by themselves; and the railway which bounds their horizon and links them with the world outside. The social environment is all-embracing: work and holidays, religous festivals, daily worship and the grim rites of death. We sense the reality of family ties, the power of the supernatural in ordinary things, the relations between the castes and between rich and poor. In creating this picture of rural Bengal, Benerji has introduced us to an area of life which so far has been a closed book to foreign visitors to India, and which scholars know little about.

This translation, which faithfully reflects the changing moods of the original as well as its many variations of style, is the work of T. W. Clark and Tarapada Mukherji, both teachers of Bengali at the School of Oriental and African Studies in the University of London. It is published as part of the translation series of the United Nations Educational, Scientific and Cultural Organizaton, and is jointly sponsored by UNESCO and the Sahitya Akademi (National Academy of Letters of India).

LONDON : GEORGE ALLEN AND UNWIN LTD